RACIAL RECONCILIATION

To Morning Star Baptist Church

From Dr. Ramsey O'Daniel

11/3/14

RACIAL RECONCILIATION

RANSEY R. O'DANIEL

Tate Publishing & *Enterprises*

Racial Reconciliation
Copyright © 2009 by Ransey R. O'Daniel. All rights reserved.

This title is also available as a Tate Out Loud product. Visit www.tatepublishing.com for more information.

No part of this publication may be reproduced, stored in a retrieval system or transmitted in any way by any means, electronic, mechanical, photocopy, recording or otherwise without the prior permission of the author except as provided by USA copyright law.

Scripture quotations marked "NIV" are taken from the *Holy Bible, New International Version* ®, Copyright © 1973, 1978, 1984 by International Bible Society. Used by permission of Zondervan Publishing House. All rights reserved.

Scripture quotations marked "KJV" are taken from the *Holy Bible, King James Version*, Cambridge, 1769. Used by permission. All rights reserved.

The opinions expressed by the author are not necessarily those of Tate Publishing, LLC.

Published by Tate Publishing & Enterprises, LLC
127 E. Trade Center Terrace | Mustang, Oklahoma 73064 USA
1.888.361.9473 | www.tatepublishing.com

Tate Publishing is committed to excellence in the publishing industry. The company reflects the philosophy established by the founders, based on Psalm 68:11,
"The Lord gave the word and great was the company of those who published it."

Book design copyright © 2009 by Tate Publishing, LLC. All rights reserved.
Cover design by Cole Roberts
Interior design by Nathan Harmony

Published in the United States of America

ISBN: 978-1-60799-412-1
1. Social Science: Ethnic Studies: African American Studies
2. Social Science: Minority Studies
09.06.08

Acknowledgments

I would like to acknowledge Jesus Christ as my Lord and Savior, the author and finisher of my faith and all things. Jesus is never the author and finisher of incompleteness. Without his wisdom, knowledge, help, and love, this project would have never been completed. Second, I would like to express my gratitude to the Howard University School of Divinity for allowing me the opportunity to be part of this outstanding body of scholars and distinguished modern thinkers. Particular thanks are extended to Dr. Kortright Davis for broadening my theology and beliefs, as well as Dean Evans Crawford, Dr. Gene Rice, and Dr. Woong Joe Kang. I would also like to thank Dr. Cheryl Sanders for assisting me throughout my graduate tenure. She helped me to become a better ethicist and thinker. Also, I would like to thank all of my professors and colleagues for the many debates we conducted; they helped mold my convictions and ideology.

Third, I would like to thank Professor Rosangela Maria Vieira for opening my eyes to the problem of racism around the world. She also helped my spirituality by correcting, advising, and listening to my views regarding racism.

Finally, I would like to thank my immediate family and my congregations for their undying support and Christian love. I am indebted too, for the kindness expressed to me by all of those acknowledged here, as well as for those I might have omitted.

Introduction

This book examines issues of race relations in the United States. Its primary focus is racial reconciliation *vis-à-vis* the Christian model for human interaction. Particular emphasis will be placed on the reasons why significant progress is yet to be achieved. The United States remains essentially a polarized, stratified, and unequal nation in social, economic, and political terms. Blacks and other minorities are the primary segments affected by this reality. The development of the dissertation will propose three steps for the elimination of the existing racial divide. First, racial reconciliation should begin internally before it goes externally. Second, racial reconciliation will need to be publicized positively in the media and avidly pursued in the home. Third, racial reconciliation will have to be practiced, not just prescribed. Each race should also commit to mutual forgiveness of any unjust treatment received.

Chapter one gives a panoramic view of the existing scholarship on race relations in the United States by considering the writings of Martin Luther King Jr.; Howard Thurman; George Kelsey; Cornell West; Curtis Paul DeYoung; and J. Deotis Roberts. Chapter two deals with significant events in African American history such as the civil rights movement and the Million Man March and their significance for black spirituality, leadership, pride, and unity within the race. Chapter three examines the media and the role it plays in perpetuating stereotypes against blacks and other minorities. Also considered in this chapter is the role it plays in reinforcing ideals of race superiority, which causes division and fragmentation within the African American community. Chapter four and the conclusive statements will indicate that spirituality is the answer for racial reconciliation within the races. It will also indicate that reconciliation should be viewed as important because it helps to restore social harmony and peace. The time has come for racial reconciliation to become a reality—not just a vision—and be placed at the forefront of this generation's agenda.

An agenda that reflects racial concerns and reconciliation is present in the writing of scholars like James Cone, C. Eric Lincoln, E. Franklin Frazier, and Rosangela Maria Vieira, who have examined the plight of black peoples in light of ideals such as white supremacy, which has justified whites' subjugation of those they consider inferior to them. Cone and Frazier, for instance, have argued that racism has affected middle class African Americans nationwide. White supremacy is still a prevalent factor. It denies better opportunities in education and in the job market. Vieira surveys the plight of blacks in her native Brazil, revealing alarming similarities between the two diasporas.

While some level of progress has been achieved in the United States in areas of race recognition, the history and culture of Afro-Brazilians is not explored in the Brazilian school system. Their children do not become aware of blacks' participation in the history of their nation. Such teachings, when they occur, are imparted in total distortion, engendering in the minds of their children a misconstrued view of reality. Similarities between the Brazilian and U.S. models for race relations can also be drawn in areas of education and economic opportunities. While some segments of the black community have access to education and job opportunities in the United States, in Brazil less than two percent of blacks graduate from high school and less than one percent enter and/or complete college education. Economically speaking, they occupy the lower positions of that society. This, in a country where, according to Vieira, peoples of direct African descent represent sixty-five to seventy-eight percent of the population, is an inadmissible reality that demands serious attention and investigation. Progress has been made in areas of consciousness, with black Brazilians coming together since 1988 to challenge institutionalized racism in their country.

Likewise, racism should also be challenged in the United States, with Christians taking an active role in promoting racial reconciliation. Christ, the head of the church, advocates this idea. He proposes that his followers forgive those who have mistreated them. He offered the best example of reconciliation and forgiveness when he went to the cross. Just before he died, he said to Romans and Jews alike, "Father, forgive them, for they know not what they do" (Luke 23:34). Christ not only talked frequently about forgiveness, he demonstrated his own willingness to do so. He forgave the paralyzed man who was lowered on a stretcher through a roof, the woman caught in adultery, the woman who anointed his feet with oil, Peter for denying he knew him, and the thief on the cross.

Racial interaction and reconciliation in a context of forgiveness was offered to the woman at the well. As a Samaritan, she had an ethnic background considered inferior to that of an individual like Jesus, who originated from a Mosaic lineage. She was also viewed as a social and moral pariah because of an implied lifestyle of sexual promiscuity. To Jesus, however, she was his perfect creation, one deserving of respect and forgiveness. In light of God's forgiveness and model for racial reconciliation, humankind should be willing to reciprocate. Furthermore, reconciliation tears down many barriers, i.e., racial, social, sexual, and those of individual differences. When it is practiced, it creates progress in relationships between the races.

The Christian model for human interaction and harmony points toward forgiveness. The traditional response, however, is not the love and tolerance recommended by Jesus. Instead, many will conceal negative feelings, seek revenge, and/or turn away in hatred or resentment. This dissertation does not suggest that those who have been victimized by an unjust system passively accept the subjugation imposed upon them; rather, it proposes that importance be placed on truth, justice, and righteousness.

Meanwhile, forgiveness should, as stated, be conceded in place of revenge to those who exert aggression. The action of forgiveness creates better chances for the restoration of relationships and for the promotion of harmony within the races. When developing strategies to promote racial reconciliation, one should consider the following questions: Who will make the first move? Should whites make that first move? Will it be legitimate, or will it be just another deception? Will black men forgive white men for the rape of their mothers and sisters, perpetuated under the slavocrat system?

Will blacks forfeit financial compensation for the economic exploitation carried under slavery and beyond? Should blacks continue to reconcile with persistently and predominantly white governments? Can whites be trusted? Can blacks be trusted? What about interracial relationships? Should affairs of the heart and personal preference be considered in such interactions? How often is true love—one that mirrors Christ's love—a factor in mixed relations? Over the centuries, racial dynamics have promulgated that all that is negative is associated with blackness and—in opposition—that everything positive relates to whiteness. Does this ideology play a role in interracial relations? Are blacks marrying whites to "improve the race" or to achieve upward mobility in social, economic, and political terms, as suggested by the Latin American model?[1]

There should not be any walls of limitations impeding positive human interactions where Jesus is Lord. With teachers, preachers, theologians, and the media constantly debating racial reconciliation, why is it still a problem in the twenty-first century? People must work together to remove racial barriers between them. Tactfully negotiating individual differences should accomplish more than commands or demands. It is equally important for genuine courtesy and respect to predominate in racial dealings. An opposite posture—one of mistrust and insincerity—will only serve to hinder progress.

Furthermore, Christian theology promotes equality of peoples rather than the idea of supremacy of one race over the other. Though there are many different blood types, people live by the same blood. The finds of Dr. Charles Drew, who discovered blood plasma, indicates that whites can live using the blood of a black individual and vice versa. Humans are God's ultimate and unified creation. It is well-adjusted and devoid of discrepancies. Some may disagree, but the coherence and harmony of God's creation is an overwhelming reality that should serve as model for race relations in every civilized society. The achievement of racial harmony through reconciliation should be pursued and achieved in this country not only to restore a divine social cosmogonic order but also to insure that a better tomorrow will be in place for future generations. The United States would be improved if everyone were willing to take part in a process of racial reconciliation. This society must try to forgive and overcome racial barriers. These barriers have cost American lives and have impaired this nation in social and economic terms over the centuries. Now is the time to go beyond existing discriminatory trends to make America what it should be: one of the greatest nations on earth. The instant this dream becomes a reality, everyone will have the respect they deserve.

United States society must be willing to engage in a dialogue that will lead to reflection on what it has failed to do to promote racial reconciliation. Most people in this country reject accepting any responsibility for the failure to promote racial reconciliation. They particularly do not wish to be told how to think and act in areas of racial tolerance for the good of society. This study contends that positive leadership should be identified in each racial group. Leaders should have the boldness to speak for truth, righteousness, and justice and to encourage their community to make racial reconciliation a priority.

In the process of holding one accountable, it should be brought to the attention of this leadership that the purpose of this interaction is to restore relationships and to bring the community closer to God's ideal of peace. When arguing the plight of Africans, as well as the lack of effort they have demonstrated in promoting peace, the person doing such exhortation should exhibit a righteous attitude, even before they speak. They need to express love before bringing issues of failure to achieve racial reconciliation. They must also be willing to forgive in the same manner. Unless exhortation is tied to forgiveness, it will not help to restore relationships, but it will further divide the races. Exhortations, or rebuking, must be done in love.

> Love is patient, love is kind, love is not envious or boastful or arrogant or rude. It does not insist on its own way. It is not irritable or resentful. It does not rejoice in wrongdoing, but it rejoices in truth. It bears all things, believes all things, hopes all things, endures all things.[2]

Society in general confuses love and lust. Unlike lust, God's love is directed toward others, not toward ourselves. Love is unselfish. This love is not natural. It is possible only if God helps us set aside our own desires and instincts so we can give love, while expecting nothing in return. I believe the closer we come to Christ the more love we will show to others because Christ represents love. True love is more important than all the spiritual gifts exercised in the church body. Great faith, sacrificial giving, and miracles produce very little without love.

Genuine love makes our actions and gifts useful. Although people have different gifts, love is available to everyone.

There are three different words in Greek for love. The first word is *philos*. The word means brotherly love. Whites and blacks can learn a lot from this word. The commandment to love others is found in both the Old Testament and the New Testament. In the Christian tradition, love is not only showing respect, it is self-sacrifice and servanthood. In fact, it can be defined as "selfless giving," reaching beyond friends to enemies and persecutors alike. Furthermore, love should be the unifying force and the identifying mark of the Christian community. Maintaining and a growing relationship with God will result in growing relationships with others. Does this mean that everyone is going to like each other? Of course not, but it does mean that we will be taking a closer step toward reconciliation, particularly in racial terms.

This is the true meaning of real love because true love is an action. The greatest act of love is giving oneself for others. Martin Luther King Jr. was the prime example of putting others before himself. King went through death threats, bombed homes, mental and physical abuse, and eventually death just to exhibit the true meaning of *philos*.

The next Greek word for love is *eros*. This is the sexual love, the love between man and woman. This society has really become obsessed with sex. The media has turned the United States into a sex-oriented society. The media also preaches that immorality means freedom; however, it has been twisted, exploited, and turned into an urgent, illicit, casual and self-gratifying activity. Love has turned into lust, and lasting commitment into no strings attached. This essay supports the theology that sexual intercourse, the physical and emotional union of male and female, should be a holy means of celebrating love, producing children, and experiencing pleasure, protected by the commitment of marriage. We can infer that sex is quite important for God. The scriptures contain numerous guidelines for its use and warnings about it misuse.

The third word is *agape,* and it means unconditional love. In other words, God loves us so much that there is nothing he would not do for us. The perfect illustration of this truth is that God sent his only son into the world to save us and to show us how much he loves us. God's love is not static or self-centered. It reaches out and draws others in. God sets the pattern of true love, the basis for all love relationships. I believe that if a person loves someone dearly, they are willing to give freely to the point of self-sacrifice. God paid with the life of his son; that is the highest price he could pay. Jesus accepted our punishment, paid the price for our sins, and then offered us the new life he bought for us. It is good to know that God sent Jesus to die for us not because we were good enough but because he loved us. Why can't blacks, whites, and other races practice this same love for one another? How is it that we can go to a sports arena and be of one accord, but when we leave it is back to the same old race game again? Why is eleven o'clock on Sunday morning still the most segregated hour in the nation? How will blacks and whites get along in heaven if they cannot get along on earth?

This dissertation further examines issues related to white supremacy in the United States. Based on history, experience, and scriptures, one finds that white supremacy has played a major role in why attempts toward racial reconciliation have failed. When one race believes that it is superior to another, it causes many myths, fears, and division among humanity. This division goes back to Abram, Sarai, and Hagar. Sarai gave Hagar to Abram as a substitute wife, a common practice of that time. The primary purpose of marriage was to have children. A married woman who was sterile was shamed by her peers and was often required to give a female servant to her husband in order to produce heirs. The children born to the servant woman were considered the children of the wife. Abram was acting in line with the custom of the day, but his action showed a lack of faith that God would fulfill his promise.

Why would Sarai urge her husband to have an affair? Theologians have argued that social customs dictated the alternative solution she found to deal with her sterility. In fact, ancient laws as outlined in the Bible spelled out the procedures for Sarai's actions. However, just because it is a custom or a law does not make it right. Like Abram, Sarai had difficulty believing God's promise. Out of this lack of faith originated a series of problems. This invariably happens when people take over for God, trying to make his promise come true through efforts that are not in line with his specific directions. In this case, time was the greatest test of Abram's and Sarai's willingness to let God work in their lives. Sometimes one must wait on God because God will lift his children up in due time. When asking God for something, there is a temptation to take matters into one's own hands and interfere with God's plan. Why did Hagar despise Sarai? It is believed that Hagar realized that she was doing for her master what her mistress could not do. So she felt superior to Sarai and began to despise her. Such feelings were anticipated and implied that the servant who bore children should be punished if she presumed to be equal to her mistress.

Although Sarai arranged for Hagar to have a child by Abram, Sarai later blamed Abram for the results. It is often easier to strike out in frustration and accuse someone else than to admit an error and ask for forgiveness. Another issue that should perhaps be considered refers to why Sarai blamed Abram. Sarai was hurting emotionally and that is perhaps why she lashed out at someone close to her. She may have blamed the system, she may have blamed God for delaying his promise, or she may have blamed herself for being impatient. Instead, in her distress, she blamed her husband. Was he not the head of the family, responsible for everyone in it? Is it possible that Sarai appealed to Abram because she knew he could punish Hagar for her? Furthermore, Sarai took her anger out on Hagar and Abram. Her treatment was harsh enough to cause Hagar to run away. Anger, especially when it arises because of one's shortcomings, can be dangerous. Did Hagar deserve the treatment she received? In one sense, yes. God usually permits the law of the land to prevail, and in this ease God allowed Hagar to suffer for her superior attitude toward Sarai. Yet God cared compassionately for Hagar and her son. In fact, God blessed her with a promise similar to the one he made to Abram.

According to Genesis 16:8, Hagar was running away from her mistress and her plight. The angel of the Lord advised her to return and submit to Sarai, the cause of her distress, and to act as she should. Hagar needed to work on her attitude toward Sarai, no matter how justified it may have been. Running away from problems never solves them. It is wise to return to unpleasant circumstances, face them directly, accept God's promise of help, correct attitudes, and act as God would recommend. Should people submit to abuse? Many casekls are different, and general principles can be drawn from one biblical example. The Bible acknowledges that some

says that those who do wrong deserve retribution.[3] Hagar's actions brought on her own suffering; so does one's own. But when she obeyed God and submitted to Sarai, her change in attitude most likely brought a change in Sarai's actions. This story shows that God is willing to reconcile to humanity, regardless of its mistakes. These scriptures reveal the mistakes of these people. Sarai took matters into her own hands and gave her servant girl to Abram; Abram went along with the plan, but when circumstances began to deteriorate he refused to help solve the problem; and Hagar ran away from the problem altogether. In spite of this controversial situation, God demonstrated God's ability to work all things together for good.[4] Sarai and Abram still received the son they so desperately wanted, and God solved Hagar's problem, despite Abram's refusal to get involved. No problem is too complicated for God.

In addition, one can learn a lesson from Hagar's mistake. When God blesses God's children with a victory, they should not get egotistical and make other individuals feel less self-worth. Instead, one should humble oneself to God and to one's neighbors. Most individuals have a problem with being meek toward the other race.

The scriptures say that whoever humbles themselves will be exalted and whoever exalts themselves will be humble.[5] It has been proven in the Bible and in society that God opposes arrogant people because they rebel against him. Humility is one of the major components in one's Christian journey. Jesus is the supreme example of humility. He gave up his rights in order to obey God and to serve humankind. Like Christ's, one's attitude should be to serve out of love for God and for others, not out of guilt or fear. For this reason, the incarnation was the act of the eternally existent Son of God voluntarily assuming a human body and human nature. Without ceasing to be God, he became a human being, the man called Jesus. He did not give up his deity to become human; instead, he set aside the right to his glory and power. In submission to the Father's will, he limited his power and knowledge. Jesus of Nazareth was subject to time, space, and many other human limitations. What made his humanity unique was his freedom from sin. In his full humanity, Jesus showed us everything about God's character that can be conveyed in human terms.[6]

Also, before Jesus' days on earth, Christ enjoyed complete equality with the Father.[7] Even in human form, his essential nature remained unchanged; he was still God.[8] Yet, so that he might take away the sins of the world, he voluntarily laid aside the privileges and glory of his heavenly authority.[9] He surrendered the splendor of his position to identify with sinful humanity. Christ sets a pattern and the standard for what brings honor to God and promotes love among peoples. We should all be like-minded in our obedience to Christ and in our care for others. This is the true meaning of reconciliation. Is racial reconciliation really working? Why cannot blacks, whites, and other races relate to one another and live harmoniously?

Chapter 1

> Men often hate other because they fear each other; they fear each other because they don't know each other; they don't know each other because they cannot communicate; they cannot communicate because they are separated.
> —*Stride Toward Freedom*, Martin L. King Jr.

The comparative analysis of racial relations in a context of reconciliation have led theologians, educators, preachers, and pastors to address problematic areas despite individual differences. Racial equality, for instance, has been an issue of debate in the American economic, educational, political, social, and spiritual spheres for centuries. Will African Americans ever receive justice and equality? Will blacks and whites ever unite? Is change a dream or reality? Can Obama really bring about change? Martin L. King Jr. (1929–1968),

Howard Thurman (1900–1981), and George Kelsey (1910–1967) and other writers have attempted to deal with race relations in their writings. Each man was highly respected during the period of their struggle for social and racial justice. For example, King was outstanding for his civil rights activism, Thurman was admirable for his spirituality, and Kelsey was commendable for his ethical views. In King's book, *Where Do We Go From Here*, he proposes steps to achieve equality and emphasizes the "guaranteed annual income" as a basic attack on poverty rather than bit-by-bit programs. He argued the need for wide coalitions and continuous efforts to influence the entire political process.

King expressed the need for increased government spending for education of poor children. Employment should focus on jobs first and training later. The methods of training first and jobs later were another way of excluding blacks because it trained people for nonexistent jobs. Moreover, he was persuasive in rejecting the forces that were impeding and destroying the unity in the black and white communities to describe both national and international conflicts within the civil rights movement. He realized the lack of allies for the coalition he advocated. However, he was honest and spoke the truth about the shameful and disgraceful conditions in America. How can America be the richest country in the world while a significant number of its citizens remain impoverished? Why do racism, sexism, and classism exist in a country that stands for democracy and equality for all peoples? His action and life depicted his genuine concern for America and all of its citizens. The essence of this book emphasizes the importance of a long list of empowerment issues. King appears to feel that he cannot accept many of the programs that are being developed along new approaches since these programs point away from universal nonviolence. These programs also underscore the faith in immediate black-white cooperation and away from the ethic of universal love, which has been the pillar of King's social morality. King introduces his main argument with good rhetoric. His rejection of black power, however, seems more like rhetorical analysis.

After presenting an indisputable perspective of what black power represents, he turns to the standard stereotypes in his rejection of the concept. This seems to be a contradiction. It is as though he is not clearly outlining black power in order to make it easier to reject. However, King's nonviolent philosophy is applicable to the racial concerns. This is why his appeals for blacks to resist subjugation nonviolently, to move forward with the struggle, and to have hope *were* relevant to the masses.

In *The Luminous Darkness*, Howard Thurman effectively explains the harmful effects of segregation on black and white Americans. Thurman believes that after the government had established integration and achieved civil rights the wounds from segregation would still be raw and festering. He believes that the responsibility of hope and healing lies with the church rather than any other agency or institution. Thurman emphasizes that segregation has damaged the minds of black and white Americans tremendously. In his view, segregation gives whites a false sense of superiority and blacks a false sense of inferiority.

In addition, segregation gives whites economic, social, religious, and political privileges compared to blacks. This entire experience attacks the self-respect and personal dignity of blacks. This book is Thurman's personal interpretation of what segregation means to African Americans, whites, and to the human spirit. These words, though softly spoken, will give comfort to none of the three. Until 1954, Thurman argued the Southern white liberal willingness to improve African American's lot—better colored schools, better ghettos—so long as the system remained intact. After 1954, the liberal assisted blacks only by declaring himself an integrationist under the terms of the Supreme Court decision.

Thurman indicated that this situation opened the door to separatists. He believed that these circumstances could have been prevented by President Eisenhower. However, Eisenhower remained silent until a violent incident occurred in Little Rock. Thurman criticized the church for not providing inspirational leadership to battle segregation. He believed that the church lost the initiative to inspire the congregation to participate in the struggle against social injustice. He also believed that if the church played a significant role in addressing these poignant issues concerning race relations and reconciliation, then men would also knock at the door to inquire what was needed to become a Christian. Where is the church's voice today? Furthermore, Thurman believed that if Christians limited their practices to other Christians they would be ineffective in reversing the injustices of segregation.

In *Racism and the Christian Understanding of Man*, George Kelsey argues that racism is a form of idolatry. When Christians practice racism, it makes them disloyal to the Christian faith. The doctrine of racism not only segregates man from God, it also detaches man from himself.

Therefore, he knows not who he is, nor is he able to affirm his self-identity. This predicament
of man can be overcome only by his returning to and keeping his faith in God. In this book, Kelsey showed his ability to reason with great theologians. He argues that racism was built into the structure of the American society from its very genesis. For this reason, a large number of American Christians do not understand the secular nature of the racist structures prevalent in this society. In essence, Kelsey believes that racists deceive themselves since it gives them a false sense of superiority. He gained tremendous respect among theologians as a superb interpreter of Christian ethics. Kelsey questions the reasons why most churchgoing Christian Americans still practice race prejudice and racial discrimination and systematically evade issues of racial reconciliation. I feel that eleven o'clock on Sunday mornings is still the most segregated hour in the United States. I wonder why that is.

Martin L. King Jr.; Howard Thurman; and George D. Kelsey aimed at viewing issues of race relation and racial reconciliation from a Christian perspective. They explained the responsibilities of Christians in reference to interactions. They tried to illustrate to white Christians that it was their duty to negate the wrong that their forefathers had done to African Americans. These authors contend that racism, segregation, and hatred have plagued America for years. The founding fathers built this country upon racism. Some were slaveholders themselves, and others institutionalized racism through the laws they enacted and passed to justify slavery. Unfortunately, some white Christian preachers referenced scriptures to justify slavery and the mistreatment of blacks. However, there were a remnant of whites who opposed slavery. Such whites were William Wilberforce; William Lloyd Garrison; John Brown, who sacrificed his sons to abolish slavery; and many more. If it had not been for a small number of whites, Harriet Tubman could not have freed as many slaves as she did. She had the heart, but whites had the food and houses to hide the slaves and keep them from being caught. This is why King, Thurman, and Kelsey discussed the racial problems from a Christian perspective—because it transcended man's theology. Each man knew and acknowledged that racism was a serious problem in America. They knew that this was a way of life for some white Americans. As a result, each gave a unique theology, but freedom was a similar objective.

Though King was known as a civil rights leader, theologian, and author, his background, knowledge, and heritage originated from the traditional black church. He was born on Jan. 15, 1929 in Atlanta, Georgia to the Rev. Martin Luther King Sr. and Mrs. Alberta King. He attended both public elementary and high schools and the private Laboratory High School of Atlanta University. At age fifteen, King entered Morehouse College as a special student. He graduated from Morehouse in 1948 and enrolled in Crozer Theological Seminary the fall semester of 1948.

Three years later, he graduated with high honors and was the winner of the J. Lewis Crozer postgraduate fellowship. King then earned a PhD in Systematic Theology from Boston University in 1955. His dissertation was entitled, "A Comparison of the Conceptions of God in the Thinking of Paul Tillich and Henry Nelson Wieman." During his last year of doctoral studies, Thurman joined the faculty of Boston

University. The spiritual and moral energy Thurman generated influenced King greatly. Both displayed exceptional spiritual and moral energy and were academically astute. Thurman was known for his mysticism and King for his oratorical skills. Both were advocates for democracy, freedom, and justice for all. Additionally, Gandhi influenced both men.

Howard Thurman was a preacher, teacher, scholar, author, poet, and mystic. He was a leading light of the black intellectual community in the twentieth century. Although he did not receive similar publicity as King in the civil rights movement, he was an inspiration to the movement. He helped introduce the ideals of nonviolence that came from the Indian nationalist Mahatma Gandhi to the civil rights movement. Thurman worked in the background constructing a theology that would reconcile the races in the struggles of the civil rights period with the spiritual concerns of the church.

Thurman was born in Daytona, Florida in 1900. Unlike King, he was raised poor. His father died when he was seven, and his grandmother cared for him. Like King, Thurman attended a public elementary school in Daytona Beach. Daytona was a strictly segregated city. It provided no schooling for black children beyond the seventh grade. This was a year short of the requirement for admission to enter high school. Without an eighth grade, there could be no demand for a black high school. If by chance they made a demand, they could be denied on the basis that black children were not qualified. This sort of action is pitiful and demonstrates hatred and selfishness. However, his academic potential impressed the principal of the black elementary schools, and he volunteered to teach Thurman the eighth grade material. After tutoring Thurman, the principal informed the superintendent that he had a boy who was ready to take the eighth grade test. The superintendent agreed to let him take the test on one condition. The condition was that he examined Thurman himself. Thurman passed and a short time later the eighth grade level was added to the black public schools. Although Thurman earned an eighth grade diploma, he departed Daytona because the city did not have a black public high school. As a result, he went to a church-supported high school in Jacksonville, Florida. While boarding a train to Jacksonville, his trunk did not have any handles and was tied shut with a rope. Therefore, it could not be checked as baggage and was sent as freight at an extra charge. Thurman sat on the station steps and began crying in frustration. A black man dressed in overalls asked him what was the trouble. When Thurman explained, the man went to the ticket agent, paid the freight charge, and walked away. Where is the unity in the black community today? What changed? Why are blacks killing blacks? Thurman never learned the man's name or saw him again. This exemplifies the unity that blacks once had.

Thurman graduated as class valedictorian in 1919. This accolade won him a scholarship

to Morehouse College in Atlanta, Georgia where he majored in economics. Because of his interest in religion and philosophy, he became a licensed Baptist preacher at the age of twenty-one. In the spring of 1923, Thurman graduated with honors and applied to Colgate-Rochester Theological Seminary in New York. The school had a strict racial quota: no more than two black students were admitted in each class. This was Thurman's firsthand experience with segregation. Although his white classmates accepted him, there were many small incidents that reminded him that he was a black man in a predominantly white, racist society.

Thurman's belief in the universality of the Christian message of love was sometimes tested. Nevertheless, his experience at Rochester served to confirm his ideology that the "magnetic field of ethical awareness" must be extended to everyone. He carried this belief throughout his life. While at Colgate-Rochester Seminary, Thurman and two white students, Red Matthews and Dave Voss, became good friends for life. He was ordained that summer after his first year in the seminary. In 1926, Thurman graduated first in his class and accepted a position as pastor of a black Baptist church in Oberlin, Ohio. His reputation as an outstanding preacher spread rapidly. Both blacks and whites became members of his congregation, in a rare demonstration of unity. Why not now? This was almost unheard of in America at this time. In the fall of 1929, Thurman was offered a teaching post at Morehouse and Spelman Colleges. This is where he began to apply his religious insight to social concerns.

His discussions with students at Morehouse aroused his thinking to the maximum capacity. They discussed central issues of self-realization as black men in American society. They asked questions such as: Why are we in college? What are we trying to find? How can we immunize ourselves against the destructive aspects of this environment? How can we manage the fear of the white man's power and not be defeated by our own rage and hatred? It was during this time that he wrote his first book, *Deep River*.

In 1932, while President Mordecai Johnson was striving to build a community of first-rate black scholars, Thurman moved to the School of Religion at Howard University. He became a social ethics teacher and dean of Rankin Chapel. Ralph Bunch, Carter G. Woodson, and Benjamin Mays were among those on the faculty. In 1935, Thurman and his wife were blessed with the opportunity to visit India. There, he spoke to Hindus, Muslims, and Buddhists who challenged him to defend Christianity because they did not comprehend his optimism about the same religion the oppressors practiced. The climax of the journey to India was Thurman meeting with Gandhi. They conversed at the Indian leader's Ashram, discussing their struggle for independence and the African American struggle for equality. This led Thurman to introduce nonviolence to the civil rights struggle.

Thurman returned to Howard until 1944 and then to Boston University, where he retired in 1965. He served as the dean of March Chapel, a position held by no other African American. As professor of spiritual discipline and resources, Thurman devoted his life to being a spiritual counselor. His students included Martin Luther King Jr.; Whitney Young; Samuel Proctor; Vernon Jordan; Otis Moss; and Jesse Jackson. For this reason, Thurman is known as a leader of leaders and preacher of preachers.

George Kelsey was born on July 24, 1910 in Columbus, Georgia. Though he supported King and Thurman, he approached the racial problem from an ethical point of view. Kelsey also was a preacher and an educator and a professor of Christian ethics. He graduated from Morehouse College in 1934 and from Andover Newton Theological School in 1937. He later earned a Ph.D. from Yale University in 1946. Kelsey served as professor of religion and philosophy at Morehouse

College from 1938–45. After this position, he taught Christian ethics at Drew University and became a nationally known ethicist. His works made a significant contribution to the racial problem in America. Kelsey claims that racism is a faith. It is a form of idolatry. According to him, the purpose of *Racism and Christian Understanding of Man* was to provide a Christian criticism of racism as a faith system. He believed that Christians failed to recognize racism as an idolatrous faith, one that is characterized by total hostility. Thurman and Kelsey agree that segregation is not of God.

James Sellers, who wrote *The South and Christian Ethics*, disagrees with Thurman and Kelsey. Sellers argues that God ordained segregation and it is a religious issue. Kelsey states that Sellers' ideas are inconsistent because segregation is religious but it is not a religious issue.

The author's meaning, I think, is this: segregation is religious, all right, but it is not a religious issue. An issue is something you can argue about. Segregation, on the other hand, is so God-ordained, and therefore religious, that it is not a question.[10]

In addition, racism and segregation are central to a plan of political and economic action by racists. Racism is an oppressive and brutal system. It serves to control and destroy. White Americans have used this system consistently to keep blacks subjugated. History shows that white America has benefited economically for decades by this system. They worked blacks for years without pay. During the Reconstruction period, whites promised blacks forty acres and a mule. However, due to racism, blacks never received any compensation.

Kelsey contends that the Christian doctrine is one of equality. It relies on genuine faith.

It is not a perception of sight. Christianity is an affirmation of faith because it relies solely on God and not men. The premises of this study agree with Kelsey's views that men and women are equal because God has created them in God's own image. Kelsey helps us to understand that there is evidence in history that men and women are unequal in knowledge, skill, power, and cultural achievements overall. When the Christian faith speaks of equality, it refers to the action and purpose of God. Christianity affirms the unity of humankind, as underscored in Kelsey's following statement:

> The religious belief in the unity of the human race through the Creation, in and for the Divine images, is completely independent of all biological, palaeontological, scientific results. The story of Adam in Genesis expresses, in historical form, it is true, a fact which in itself is super-empirical and super-historical; the biological, genealogical question has very little to do with belief in the unity of the creation…The unity of the divine creation of man lies upon a quite different plane. Humanity is not necessarily a unity from a zoological point of view; it may indeed be composed of different species of differing origin or it may not. It is, however, beyond all doubt a unity, a humanitas, 'through' the humanism, its one origin and its one destiny in God's creative Word and plan of salvation, spiritually given to man by God himself.[11]

The African slave trade was, in effect, a great episode in genocide. It has been implied that for every one African that made it to the American shores, three or four perished under the brutality of the African slave trade. Hitler used genocide to exterminate Jews. Does black America practice genocide by selling drugs to each other? Can we as humans stop genocide? If so, why does it exist? George Kelsey gives an accurate definition for racism: Genocide is the ultimate form of racism—the active desire to eliminate a culture based solely on their race.

> Racism is a faith. It is a form of idolatry... In its early modern beginnings, racism was a justificatory devise. It did not emerge as a faith. It arose as an ideological justification for the constellation of political and economic power which was expressed in colonialism and slavery. But gradually the idea of the superior race was heightened and deepened in meaning and value so that it pointed beyond the historical structures of relation, in which it emerged, to human existence itself.[12]

Ruth Benedict also defines racism as:

> The dogma that one ethnic group is condemned by nature to hereditary inferiority and another group is destined to hereditary superiority. It is the dogma that the hope of civilization depends upon eliminating some races and keeping others pure. It is the dogma that one race has carried progress throughout human history and can alone ensure future progress.[13]

Racism is a system of power. This power denies people jobs, opportunities, and complete freedom. Where do we go from here? Is it chaos or community? The status of the American society is chaos. Racism, sexism, and classism are issues that we face as a race and as a nation. Since racism exists and the system has held back blacks, I believe that the government is obligated to eradicate racism, sexism, and classism by all means—either through free education, reparation, or tax exemption. This will compensate for the act of chattel slavery. Slavery is a crime, or is it? If so, someone is liable for the crime. Reparation is a frightening word to the government because it is repaying African Americans the debt owed them for slavery. I feel that reparation means to give servants what they are worth. In essence, this is what King, Thurman, and Kelsey wanted for African Americans. They loved and believed in America, though they did not like her racist customs.

These men had more similarities than differences. These differences, however, did not keep them from fighting racism and segregation. For example, King's book, *Where Do We Go From Here,* argues for the need of wide coalitions and continuous efforts to influence the entire political process from the selection of candidates to election day. This book dealt with civil rights and political issues that were relevant to the African American. King's position seemed to be impeccable in theory, but it suffered from the lack of available allies for the coalition he advocated. Can poor whites in America be brought to recognize their compatibility with the American Negro? Dr. King approached this racial problem not only from a preacher/pastor perspective but from a community activist approach.

The Luminous Darkness, unlike *Where Do We Go From Here,* addresses racial problems from a spiritual perspective. This book is a personal testimony concerning the crippling effects of racial segregation on the human spirit. Thurman did not direct his readers to get involved in politics as King did. Rather, he testifies on the grounds of hope for Negroes and whites, stating that:The grounds were as follows: limitations imposed on the Negro are in violation of the Constitution; as the African Americans gradually lose their fear of the power of the white man, the white man will fear for his own security, and may seek all possible ways to remove it; in a changing world segregation cannot survive in modern life.

They were proponents of education, economic expansion, and Christianity. Each individual offered insight into the issue of racism from an ethical point of view. Though Christians, they were not perfect. However, they tried to live righteously. King, Thurman, and Kelsey understood salvation. They realized that it was the work of grace made possible through the life, death, suffering, and resurrection of Jesus Christ, the Lord, Savior, and Redeemer of humankind. It is lamentable that hate groups like the Klan and others use Christianity to justify their racist views. Some theologians, like James Sellers, have written literature claiming that blacks are inferior to whites. This has led to the miseducation of whites and blacks. In schools of theology, whites and blacks were taught by people who justified segregation. This is a part of American history. Racist whites have designed the educational system in America to belittle the contributions made by African Americans to this country. The aim was to transform blacks into puppets of a Eurocentric sham. Racist teachers did not tell students that ancient African ancestors knew science to prepare poisons for arrowheads, to mix colors for paintings, and to extract metals from nature, as underscored by E. A. Wallis Budge in *The Book of the Dead*. Very little was said about the chemistry in the method of Egyptian embalming, which was the product of the Northern Africans.

The educational system has miseducated blacks. Blacks have been taught that we came from slaves instead of kings. There is a difference between a black person and a Negro. A black is a person who thinks for himself or herself. A Negro is a person who conforms to the world or lets others think for him or for her. Some Negroes will disagree with this theology because they place their belief in a racist educational system. King, Thurman, and Kelsey have illustrated a means to combat racism through educational, political, spiritual, and financial means. *Racism and the Christian Understanding of Man* added a discussion from a scientific outlook. The author's descriptions of the racist point of view are designed with scholarly restraint. His analysis of the Christian perspective is informed by the biblical message interpreted by the Niebuhrs, Barth, Buber, Ruth Benedict, R.K. Merton, G.E. Simpson, J.M. Yinger, and Gunnar Myradal.

According to Kelsey, racism is a decisive act of turning away from God. It is life according to the flesh. Can a racist be a Christian? The lives of King, Thurman, and Kelsey exemplified concerns for a heavenly reality more than a earthly one. These men were Christian first and black second. Jesus was their Lord and Savior. Each man spoke the truth of love, courage, and care for the poor. Their Christian faith and political outlooks influenced many people toward an ethical behavior. The teachings of the apostle Paul and Jesus Christ prompted the ethical conduct of these men and me. What about you? Their spiritual intensity motivated them to continue pressing toward the mark of the high calling of God. They encountered many circumstances such as racism, segregation, and deceitful blacks. Nevertheless, they remained focused. Thurman and Kelsey's books did not offer alternatives to the race problem, nor did they offer a five or ten-point plan to eliminate racial issues or to promote racial reconciliation in this society. King, on the other hand, does offer such a plan; he calls it guaranteed income. Thurman and Kelsey's theories for solutions of racism in the United States are nearly flawless, but they could include of financial reparations for the institution of slavery since whites worked black ancestors for years for little to no pay. This is a debt and a crime; something has to be done because it is wrong!

Cornell West, J. Deotis Roberts, and Curtis P. DeYoung have addressed the racial problem from several perspectives. They addressed it from scholarly, educational, and biblical point of views. West was born on June 2, 1953, in Tulsa, Oklahoma, the grandson of the Rev. Clifton L. West, Sr., pastor of the Tulsa Metropolitan Baptist Church. West's mother, Irene Bias West, was an elementary school teacher (and later principal), while his father, Clifton L. West, was a civilian Air Force administrator. West claims that he received dignity, integrity, majesty, and humility from his parents. These values presented to him the Christian narratives and ethical views. According to West, the basic for his life vocation lies in three components of the Christian doctrine, which are a gospel with emphasis on love and social applications, humility, and humane concern for others while having a political consciousness that will strive for justice.

J. Deotis Roberts was born in Spindate, North Carolina,

on July 12, 1927. He was educated at Johnson C. Smith University, Shaw University, Hartford Seminary Foundation, and the University of Edinburgh. He did further studies at Cambridge University, and he has held major study fellowships from the Lilly Foundation, the Ford Foundation, and the Association of Theological Schools. Those fellowships have enabled him to examine many religions while traveling to numerous countries in Europe, Asia, and Africa. He also studied at Harvard Divinity University, Duke University, the University of Chicago, and Michigan State University. His concern has been in the area of comparative theology. He maintains an interest in the broad scope of religion and endeavors to understand it in the context of particularity and universality. As a result of this wide exposure to other religious traditions and in view of his own theological orientation, Roberts seeks to develop a black theology from a more inclusive perspective than did James Cone.

Curtis Paul DeYoung demonstrated racial reconciliation by marrying a black woman, and he holds a B.A. in religion from Anderson University, Anderson, Indiana, and a Master of Divinity from Howard University School of Divinity in Washington, DC. DeYoung once served as the pastor in the Church of God denomination. Currently, he is the Executive Director of TURN Leadership Foundation in Minneapolis, Minnesota, an urban resourcing network committed to working for reconciliation and social justice across racial, cultural, ecumenical, gender, and economic lines. DeYoung demonstrates a courageous call to Christian unity that does not dismiss the multicultural issues. His claim is greatly empowered by his ability to discern and communicate what the Bible teaches about the oneness of humanity in light of the gospel of Jesus Christ. His work provides Christians with a principal that addresses racial, ethnic, and cultural diversity from a biblical perspective. "The Bible addresses issues of diversity, but not by starting with the difference in the human family."

West, who is a professor at Harvard University, is known nationwide for his analytical speeches and writings on issues of morality, race relations, cultural diversity, and progressive politics. As a scholar, activist, and teacher of religion, he recapitulates his theological concerns with his political opinions. His philosophy and "on-the-streets" politics reflect his passion and commitment to his main goal for the freedom of blacks in America. For this reason, Henry Louis Gates has called West our black Jeremiah. In *Race Matter*, Cornell West critiques the cultural, spiritual, and racial crisis confronting America today. West acknowledges that the economic decline, cultural chaos, and racial conflicts are problematic in America. He places the spiritual reduction as the head of all problems in America.

In West's view, and that of this author, spirituality is a major component in this society and should be placed at the top of this country's agenda. According to West, the loss of hope, the absence of self-love and love of others, and the breakdown of family and neighborhood bonds has led to the social separation from one's environment and the cultural erosion of the black community. Consequently, this hopelessness affects black children directly, thus impacting their future negatively. Spirituality has helped African Americans to maintain sanity in an insane world. Had it not been for spirituality, oppressed people worldwide would not have been able to subsist. It is spirituality that sustains the oppressed, helping them to face despair and disease and to keep their dignity and decency in a racist world. Spirituality also allows oppressed people to overcome the forces determined to maintain them at the periphery of a system where they are systematically humiliated and denied opportunities. Given a chance, spirituality could help change the structures of racist orders and the minds of those controlling and enacting their discriminatory dictums. For instance, police would not assume that every black man is a criminal as observed in police racial profiling as observed in the following instance described by West:

> Ugly racial memories of the past flashed through my mind. Years ago, while driving from New York to teach at Williams College, I was stopped on fake charges of trafficking cocaine. When I told the police officer I was a professor of religion, he replied, "Yeh, and I'm the Flying Nun. Let's go, nigger."[14]

West's insight on nihilism in black America provides his readers with enlightening assertions on racial reasoning, black leadership, the new black leadership, the new black conservatism, affirmative action, black-Jewish relations, Malcolm X and black rage. What is nihilism? It is a doctrine that denies reality and asserts that conditions in the social organization are so bad as to make destruction desirable for its own sake, independent of any constructive program or possibility. It also denies any objectives or real ground of truth and implies that all traditions and beliefs are illogical and that all existence is consequently senseless and useless. In West's view, nihilism is not new in America. Most African Americans believe that oppression or economic exploitation exists in this century and that nihilistic threats are one of the major enemies for African American survival in this society.

As he puts it:

> The genius of our black foremothers and forefathers was to create powerful buffers to ward off the nihilistic threat, to equip black folks with cultural armor to beat back the demons of hopelessness, meaninglessness, and lovelessness. These buffers consisted of cultural structures of meaning and feeling that created and sustained communities; this armor constituted ways of life and struggle that embodied values of service and sacrifice, love and care, discipline and excellence. In other words, traditions for blacks surviving and thriving under usually adverse New World conditions were major barriers against then nihilistic threat. These traditions consist primarily of black religious and civic institutions that sustained familial and communal networks of support.[15]

Nevertheless, there is a cure for nihilism. It is love and care. Love is greater than any power on this earth. Self-love and the love of others are essential in attempting to deal with nihilism and racism. Jesus believed that love must be at the center of an individual's heart. J. Deotis Roberts' ideas are effective among Christians because love and reconciliation are the nucleus of his theology. In *Liberation and Reconciliation,* J. Deotis Roberts implies that reconciliation and liberation are interrelated. Roberts also places emphasis on redemptive suffering. He makes a valid point by stating that redemptive suffering carries a special ethical responsibility for reconciliation. Reconciliation is the crux of Robert's theology. He disagrees with James Cone's position of God as liberator. For instance, Roberts contends that God chose the Israelites not just to reveal that God was liberator of the oppressed, but to reveal that those who suffer unjustly were called by God to carry forth a mission of reconciliation. Roberts maintains that reconciliation requires that oppressed peoples become liberators of their plight. He argues that:

> A people chosen of God is a people who have entered a new understanding of their mission in the world. Instead of being victims of suffering, such people transmute suffering into a victory. It becomes a rod in their hand to enter into a redemptive mission among themselves and others… Upon entering into a deeper understanding of how their own lives have been purged and purified by unmerited suffering, they become a saving minority, for all men.[16]

Reconciliation is indeed a major component in Christianity. However, blacks should try to reconcile with God before reconciling with others. When blacks try to reconcile with others first, it sends a negative message to society and future generations. It may appear that blacks care more about whites than they do about themselves. Why do blacks love whites more than they love themselves? Does society value a white life more than a black life? Roberts must be careful with this theology because people may attempt to be something or someone they are not.

Cone contests on many occasions that Roberts misunderstands the meaning of Christian reconciliation. Unlike Roberts, Cone believes that reconciliation was an act of God that was implemented by Christ. Cone subscribed to the notion that God's reconciliation was an element to destroy all oppressive situations. The priority of blacks should be to liberate themselves from white racist mandates. Will blacks and whites come together? Will blacks and whites ever trust each other? If so, what will we do as a result? How will we treat each other? How will African Americans treat whites? How will African Americans treat themselves?

Blacks should place priority and strengthen relationships within the black community. Blacks must reason afrocentrically and live as blacks, not as puppets of racist white ideologies. They should not be ashamed of their African features. I feel that blacks are ashamed of their African heritage because Hollywood has portrayed Africa or African as savage and unintelligent. This is not to suggest that blacks be anti-white, but they should be proud of what God has created them to be. One may ask, Can I be both Christian and black? Martin L. King Jr. would answer yes in response because blacks and whites are equal footings. In Christ's and in King's view, we are all children of God. I agree with their beliefs. Malcolm X would answer no in response because in his opinion, "Christianity is a white man's religion," and he could not affirm a religion that is white. God created man and woman in God's image. God placed both man and woman at the pinnacle of his creation. Neither sex exalted nor is either sex depreciated. Malcolm X is correct in his assertion that some whites used Christianity to enslave blacks, but it is not a white man's religion. Christianity came from Africa and not Europe. He is right by claiming that some whites justified the killing and beating of blacks in the name of Christianity. Malcolm X, Gandhi, and others asked, "Why do blacks practice the same religion as whites?" For me, Christianity is all about forgiveness and reconciliation. God forgives me of my wrongs, so I am obligated to forgive others when they wrong me. That is love for God and humanity! Is Christianity a white man's religion? Does Christianity justify oppression?

In *Liberation and Reconciliation*, Roberts attempts to provide what he considered a missing link in Cone's theological program: reconciliation. Roberts believes that liberation and reconciliation are the two main poles of black theology. They are not antithetical; one moves naturally from one to the other in the light of Christian understanding. Roberts feels there is a theological basis for reconciliation "between equals," but he thinks that reconciliation is postrevolutionary in its direction. He is calling for a revolution in race relations with reconciliation as an essential component. Is this Christian?

Roberts also feels that whites cannot remain lieutenants in the struggle of reconciliation and liberation. They must allow blacks to set rules for themselves. Roberts and Cone agree with this philosophy. Roberts asks that whites take a more leading role in their community in preparing their neighbors to accept blacks as a people in a pluralistic society. He insists that reconciliation and liberation must come from both races—whites and blacks—as we are one body and we are joined together.

The body needs each of its parts to remain whole and meaningful. Segregation and racial divide fragments the essence of mankind. It invalidates the coherence of the divine creation. It is true that there must be a blueprint for a true Christian reconciliation. Reconciliation and liberation should not be dealt with in a futuristic time frame; they need to take place now. Reconciliation is a priority in Robert's theology. He uses 2 Corinthians 5:19 to support his views and says: "God was in Christ reconciling the world to himself."

Most black scholars who are moderate take sides with Robert's theology, and most black scholars who are militant take sides with Cone. Roberts has an issue with Cone's theology of reconciliation in that it ends and begins with blackness. Roberts feels that reconciliation is colorless. He believes that whites do not have to become blacks to be reconciled with blacks, but they must accept blacks as their equal. I agree. By this perspective, Roberts protects the integrity and humanity of both blacks and whites. When whites and blacks commit acts against each other, it is sin. Furthermore, he feels that a revolution would occur between blacks and whites in a postrevolutionary situation, which he categorizes as reconciliation. He disagrees with Cone, who denounced "whiteness" as evil and sinful. For Cone, this means that for whites to be saved they must negate themselves and become black. This will never happen because whites by nature cannot be black. They can speak, behave, and even dress like blacks, but internally they will never be black because God designed them as whites. This is not a bad thing.

Roberts asserts that blacks and whites are all one in Christ Jesus. He believes that all slave/master, servant/boss, inferior/superior relationships between blacks and whites must be abolished. True reconciliation must consist of equals. Roberts and Cone differ on the idea of the black Messiah. For instance, Roberts sees the black Messiah as a symbol or myth with a deep meaning for black oppressed peoples. Roberts is concerned about the psychological. Roberts also argues that Christ is universal. In his opinion, Christ should have the same meaning to all races as he has to blacks. One reason why he resists the idea of a black Christ is because it is exclusive. A black Christ does not include whites or others.

However, Cone makes a valid point when he contends that Jesus' blackness was based on existential commitments. In other words, Jesus is not black because of ethnicity, lineage, or geographical origin, but Jesus is black because he entered the world to relate to the poor and oppressed peoples worldwide. Nevertheless, Roberts feels that the universal Christ is particularized for the black Christian in the black experience of the black Messiah, but the black Messiah is at the same time universalized in the Christ of the gospel who meets all men in all situations. The black Messiah liberates black peoples. The universal Christ reconciles black peoples with the rest of humanity.

DeYoung discusses racial reconciliation from a different perspective. He addresses racial reconciliation from the oneness of humanity perspectives and states that:

> Unfortunately, the oneness of the human family and the universality of God's love have been distorted in post biblical times. Instead of living as one human family with many cultural expressions, we have

divided ourselves by many classifications. By way of example, the modern invention that we call "racism" created a system of racial hierarchy that undergirded the superiority of one "race" of people, white, Caucasian Europeans, for the purpose of cultural and economic domination.[17]

Why is racism still a problem in America in the twenty-first century? Will diversity be a reality or a dream? Where does racism come from? DeYoung argues that biblical interpreters intentionally manipulate the Bible to keep the Hebrews white, Northern Africa white, and Ethiopia white. For many years, blacks thought that Egyptians were white. This false interpretation has led many scholars to falsify the original biblical story. For this reason, whites have misused the Bible to stay in power and oppress people of different characteristics. The oppressor does not wish to unite with anyone. As long as there is division among blacks, white racial orders and their representatives know that they will always have power and will always control other races.

DeYoung makes good points about the biblical messages in an age of diversity. For instance, oneness of humanity is what God intended and wants. Nevertheless, one should ask the following: Will the people in power share their power with the powerless? Roberts, Cone, and DeYoung would agree that majority of whites will never share power with blacks. But what about most of the states voting for Obama? This is not a case of black victory. It is a victory for America, Democrats, and Reconciliation. DeYoung, Roberts, and West have proven that God's community is meant to be a model of justice and oneness as indicated in the following passage:

> All who believed were together and had all things in common; they would sell their possessions and goods and distribute the proceeds to all, as any had need. Day by day, as they spent much time together in the temple, they broke bread at home and ate their food with glad and generous hearts, praising God and having the goodwill of all the people. And day by day the Lord added to their number those who were being saved.[18]

Chapter 2

> I believe that it is impossible to end hatred with hatred.
> —Mahatma Gandhi

During the civil rights movement in the fifties and sixties, Dr. Martin L. King's spirituality was the driving force in his success in eliminating Jim and Jane Crowism. His love for God allowed him to accomplish things that seemed impossible. For instance, with the help of others, he broke unjust laws without resorting to violence or hatred. The first event that brought Dr. King to national attention was the Montgomery Bus Boycott in 1955. This episode came about when a young lady named Rosa Parks did not give up her seat to a white man. During this time, the metro transportation system of Montgomery, Alabama was segregated. It was legal for white passengers to sit in the front and best seats, while black passengers had to sit in the back and worse seats. Although blacks made up seventy percent of the riding population, they had to take the inferior position. Rosa Parks, who was a seamstress at that time, was tired. She had been standing all day. When the time came for her to give up her seat, she said to herself, "Enough is enough." Unfortunately, she went to jail for disobeying Montgomery's law. Fortunately, her behavior helped to destroy the segregation system.

King's thinking and theology were shaped by his beliefs in Jesus of Nazareth. This is the author's beliefs as well. He believed that justice could be achieved through love and non-violence. I do too. This is one reason why he was able to tell African Americans, in spite of the violence, bloodshed, bombing of churches, and economic exploitation, that they should love those who despitefully use them. They also should pray for those who curse them, and turn the other cheek to those who use physical brutality toward them. Martin practiced this belief during his tenure here on this earth.

Nevertheless, King's spirituality allowed him to be a man of protest. During his first major speech at Holt Street Baptist Church, December 5, 1955, King told an audience of nearly five thousand African Americans:

> We are not wrong in what we are doing. If we are wrong, then the Supreme Court of this nation is wrong. If we are wrong, the Constitution of the United States is wrong. If we are wrong, God Almighty is wrong. If we are wrong, Jesus of Nazareth was merely a utopian dreamer and never came down to earth. If we are wrong, justice is a lie … And we are

> determined here in Montgomery to work and fight until justice runs down like water and righteousness like a mighty stream.[19]

King wanted the blacks to know that there was not anything wrong with them protesting for righteousness. He believed that this protest was a constitutional right as well as a biblical principle. Similarly, racial reconciliation is a biblical principle as well.

King also drew upon the difference between love and justice he found in the theological writings of Paul Tillich and Reinhold Niebuhr. At the beginning of King's tenure, he clearly made love secondary to justice, as observed in the following statement:

> I want to tell you this evening that it is not enough to talk about love. Love is one of the principal parts of the Christian faith. There is another side called justice... Justice is love correcting that which would work against love. The Almighty God... is not... just standing out saying, 'Behold thee, I love you, Negro.' He's also the God that standeth before the nations and says: 'Be still and know that I am God, that if you don't obey me I'm gonna break the backbone of your power...' Standing beside love is always justice. And we are only using the tools of justice. Not only are we using the tools of persuasion but we've got to use the tools of coercion.[20]

Most people have interpreted King's central message as love, but when King first started out as the president of Montgomery Improvement Association, his theme was justice because he insisted that black people should stand up and demand their rights in this country for themselves, for their neighbors, and for the sake of humanity. It was after he was introduced to Mahatma Gandhi's message of nonviolence and had matured spiritually and mentally in the civil rights struggle that love became his central theme.

Furthermore, nonviolence was not a new idea. A white abolitionist, William Lloyd Garrison, made an attempt to use nonviolence as an instrument of liberation during slavery. King and Gandhi used the same phase Garrison used:

> "The history of mankind is crowded with evidences proving that physical coercion is not adapted to moral regeneration; that the sinful disposition of man can be subdued only by love; that evil can be exterminated from the earth only by goodness; that there is great security in being gentle, harmless, long-suffering, and abundant in mercy; that it is only the meek who shall inherit the earth, for the violent who resort to the sword are destined to perish with the sword."[21]

There have always been whites of good will on the side of the oppressed. Which side are you on? Nonviolent activities, such as sit-ins, boycotts, and mass marches were very effective in fighting the government with its unjust laws. Evidence proves it.

Nevertheless, King advocated that love expressed in a nonviolent protest was the only means of achieving justice, which he associated with desegregation. According to King's theology, there was a close interrelationship between love and justice. For instance, love was tied to integration while justice was related to the political demonstration.

Meanwhile, King urged his followers to accept nonviolence as a way of life. He expressed to them that even if they could not accept nonviolence as an affirmation of faith, then they should accept it as a practical way of achieving justice in America. King declared that violence would not achieve freedom for African Americans; it would get a whole lot of them killed and serve as an excuse for whites not to do anything about oppression, racism, and injustice.

In contrast to Malcolm X, who argued that nonviolence disarmed the oppressed, Martin maintained that it disarmed the oppressor. As King stated, nonviolence weakens his morale and exposes his defenses. And at the same time it works on his conscience. And he just doesn't know what to do. As he puts it:

> In addition, King told a group of African Americans: "Now I can assure you, that if we rose up in violence in the South, our opponents would really know what to do, because they know how to operate on this level. They are experts on violence. They control all the forces of violence. But nonviolence confounds the oppressor. If he beats you, you develop the power to accept it without retaliating. If he beats you, fine. If he throws you in jail in the process, you go on in there and transform the jail from a dungeon of shame to a haven of freedom and human dignity. Even if he tries to kill you, you develop the quiet courage of dying if necessary without killing. The oppressor ends up frustrated. This is the power of nonviolence."[22]

According to King and the believers of the nonviolent philosophy, nonviolence was neither a sign of weakness nor a lack of courage because only the strong could be nonviolent because it would be easy to turn to violence. In fact, King directed people not to get involved in the movement unless they had the strength, faith, and courage to accept brutality without retaliating.

Consequently, King would ask, "How could a ten percent Negro minority with no access to the weapons of warfare ever expect to wage a successful revolution against a white majority with the military technology of the United States?"[23] In King's opinion, this was nothing but a case of generational suicide.

King, a man of visions and dreams, was known as The Dreamer. His purpose in the movement was to bring into existence his dream of equality, freedom, and justice for all of God's children. As he states,

> We are seeking to bring into full realization the American dream—a dream yet unfilled. A dream of equality, of privilege and property widely distributed; a dream of a land where men no longer argue that the color of a man's skin determines the content of his character; the dream of a land where every man will respect the dignity and worth of human personality—this is the dream. When it is realized, the jangling discords of our nation will be transformed into a beautiful symphony of brotherhood, and men everywhere will know that America is truly the land of the free and the home of the brave.[24]

On August 28, 1963, King delivered his famous "I Have a Dream" speech, which reads as follows.

> I am happy to join with you today in what will go down in history as the greatest demonstration for freedom in the history of our nation. A great beacon of light of hope which Lincoln's Emancipation Proclamation gave to Negro slaves who had been seared in the flames of withering injustice. But one hundred years later, the Negro still is not free, but is sadly crippled by the manacles of segregation and the chains of discrimination living on a lonely island of poverty in the midst of a vast ocean of material prosperity. America has not lived up to its promise-of-freedom-to-Negro-people who were given a bad check; a check which has come back marked insufficient funds. But we refuse to believe that the bank of justice is bankrupt. King challenged everyone to make the U.S. government cash the check that would bring the riches of freedom and the security of justice to all its citizens. That was why he said that we have … come to this hallowed spot to remind America … that now is time to rise from the dark and desolate valley of segregation to the sunlit path of racial justice. I have a dream today. I have a dream that one day … right there in Alabama, little black boys and black girls will be able to join hands with little white boys and white girls as sisters and brothers. I have a dream that one day every valley shall be exalted, every hill and mountain shall be made low. The rough places will be plain and the crooked places will be made straight, and the glory of the Lord shall be revealed, and all flesh shall see

it together. Let freedom from the prodigious hilltop of New Hampshire; let freedom ring from the mighty mountains of New York; let freedom ring from the heightening Alleghenies of Pennsylvania; let freedom ring from the snowcapped Rockies of Colorado; let freedom ring from curvaceous slopes of California. But not only that. Let freedom ring from Stone Mountain of Georgia; let freedom ring from Lookout Mountain of Tennessee; let freedom ring from every hill and molehill of Mississippi. From every mountainside, let freedom ring. And when this happens, and when we allow freedom to ring, when we let it ring from every village and every hamlet, from every state and every city, we will be able to speed up that day when all of God's children, black men and white men, Jews and Gentiles, Protestants and Catholics, will be able to join hands and sing in the words of the old Negro spiritual: Free at last. Free at last. Thank God Almighty, we are free at last.[25]

Most of the people and King left Washington that day with high expectations of brotherhood and sisterhood between blacks and whites in this country. Most thought that the dream was becoming a reality. However, among the skeptics was Malcolm X, who believed that white America could not be changed through an appeal to the conscience. In fact, Malcolm called the March on Washington a circus, stating that he did not see America as a dream; he saw it as a nightmare.

In a sense, Malcolm was right because two weeks after the "March on Washington," the Sixteenth Baptist Church in Birmingham, Alabama, was bombed and four little girls were killed. Nevertheless, King's spirituality refused to allow his hopes for reconciliation to be shattered. In eulogizing three of the girls, he said, "These children…were the victims of one of the most vicious, heinous crimes ever perpetrated against humanity."[26] However, he was certain that their deaths were not in vain. Instead of causing him to doubt his dream, this violent act gave him more hope because he believed that their deaths would serve as a redemptive force that would bring light to an opaque country.

King's spirituality allowed him to be a preacher as well as a man who would stand in the forefront of the struggle and face constant death threats, blackmail, and political humiliation. Also, his spirituality enabled him to stand strong and challenge the black nationalists who were becoming popular. Setting the captives free, uplifting the poor, and doing the will of God were King's top priorities during his reign as a national leader. His call for a nonviolent posture was revolutionary, and it touched many people during his stand for justice, equality, and freedom. King was able to bring together people of all races, as well as educated and uneducated people, because he depended on soul force rather than physical force.

Meanwhile, Malcolm X's spirituality allowed him to stand as a Black Nationalist leader and speak the truth about racists, racism, and hypocrisy. For instance, he identified whites as the ones who are most responsible for the suffering of black peoples. Malcolm believed that whites manipulated blacks into the terrible conditions blacks were in. Unemployment, underemployment, dirty streets, rat and roach-infested tenements, pimping and prostituting, drug pushing and dope addition, black-on-black crimes, and police brutality were all controlled by white folks. Nevertheless, Malcolm criticized blacks for accepting these conditions. Malcolm was particularly critical of the civil rights leaders because he felt that they allowed themselves to be used by the enemy: white oppressive orders and their representatives.

During the beginning of Malcolm's leadership, and due to the interest of unity, he avoided name-calling because he and Elijah Muhammad thought that it would put walls between them and black leaders. But later on in his rank as a national leader, he would speak openly against the civil rights leaders. Malcolm would refer to them as old, white-minded, brainwashed, handkerchief-head Negroes. Also, he called them "Negro stooges."[27] Malcolm stated that these Negroes were nothing but modern "Uncle Toms." For instance, according to Malcolm, these Negroes who were usually well-dressed and well-educated represented another culture and not their own. They spoke with an Ivy League college accent. They were known as Doctor, Professor, Attorney, Reverend, or Reverend Doctor. Since King was the symbol of the civil rights movement and the one whom whites promoted as the leader of blacks, Malcolm X singled him out as a special object of criticism. "The white man is our first and main enemy. Our second enemy is the Uncle Toms, such as Martin Luther King and his turn the other cheek method."[28] Malcolm called King a "religious Uncle Tom, a traitor, a chump, and the Rev. Dr. Chickenwing."[29] However, Martin never responded back in that type of manner. Malcolm's blunt speaking was painful to whites, but poor blacks readily welcomed his message because it gave them hope and pride.

Several blacks felt that Malcolm was speaking the truth, but the way he said it sounded like hate, so the media used it to their advantage. Also, most of the blacks were afraid to say what Malcolm was saying. Malcolm used the street rallies not only to increase the membership of the Nation of Islam, but also to infuriate whites with his angry rhetoric. For instance, he would call them blue-eyed devils, white apes, and white beasts. Also, he would use the analogy of a fox and a wolf to describe whites. He paralleled the whites who lived up north with the fox because he said they were sneaky. He associated the whites who lived down south with the wolf because he said they would let you know where you stand. This rhetoric helped Malcolm by getting him attention and building up the Nation of Islam, but it hurt his image, and the government and the media used it to confuse and further divide him and black leaders.

Although the media tried to portray Malcolm as a negative black-nationalist leader, most poor blacks believed that Malcolm would never sell them out or sell them down the river for status or money. At the beginning of Malcolm's profession, most of his following were the poor and downtrodden. As time progressed, he had some influential people agreeing with him as well. For instance, Alex Haley, James Baldwin, Maya Angelou, James Farmer, C. Eric Lincoln, and others were willing to listen to his opinions and beliefs. During the writing of Malcolm's autobiography, Alex Haley provided impressions of Malcolm being a father, husband, and a friend that contradicted the image the media had portrayed him to be.

James Baldwin stated that toward the end, "there was practically no difference between them." Baldwin embraces the fateful experience of both Malcolm and Martin—however divergent their paths, ambitions, stances, strategy—to illuminate the condition of being black in America.

Maya Angelou met Malcolm in 1961 to get his opinion of the assassination of the Congolese Prime Minister, Patrice Lumumba. She described Malcolm as a young man with dignity, intelligence, nobility, graciousness, warmth, courage, compassion, fearlessness, sincerity, cunning, imagination, charisma, and good looks. Whether an individual liked Malcolm or not, it was obvious that he had intelligence, courage, and charisma.

Martin and Malcolm's spirituality impressed millions even though they had different oratorical styles, strategies, and beliefs. By the power of their God, they were able to inform and persuade millions in a positive direction. Since Martin was well-educated and quite successful in the white man's world, he was optimistic about white people and believed that a change was going to take place. Also, Martin believed that eventually justice and freedom would come to everyone, regardless of their race or status. On the other hand, Malcolm was self-educated and was pessimistic about whites and the government in this country. There was no positive experience in Malcolm's childhood that gave him affirmative reasons to support the idea that whites were people of good will. In addition, he argued that whites would never share their power and privilege with the oppressed blacks in their society.

Martin's dream was influenced by his social heritages, while Malcolm's nightmare affected his life. These heroes came from different backgrounds of class, familial support, political tradition, geography, religious tradition, and education. Nevertheless, that did not stop them from approaching the black freedom struggle and reconciliation. Malcolm's idea of justice differed from Martin's. For instance, Martin, being a Christian, believed in Jesus' command to love the enemy. Malcolm, being Muslim, believed in the eye for eye, a tooth for tooth, an arm for arm, head for head, and a life for life philosophy. Even though Malcolm was more famous for his critique of whites, his call for unity among blacks was actually the main theme of his ministry. He believed that if blacks were going to achieve freedom, then they must replace self-hate with the love of themselves.

Malcolm told blacks that they were culturally dead, alienated from their past and one another. This was the reason why blacks did not love each other and could not achieve the unity that was necessary for their freedom. He suggested that they should not even think about uniting with others or loving anybody else until they first learned how to come together with love and respect to one another. This philosophy is still true today. How can you love somebody else if you do not love yourself? Blacks still have problems with self-love and unity in the black community. African Americans need to be re-educated. Most blacks need to learn to love one another, while most whites need to understand how to love blacks. Blacks, on the other hand, do not have to learn how to love whites because they already love them wholeheartedly. Blacks marry whites. They try to talk like whites, and they even try to act like them.

Many people tried to debate Malcolm concerning his separatist views, but they were not successful. For instance, James Farmer and Bayard Rustin were two of his opponents who believed in integration. Farmer and Rustin admitted that even though Malcolm's message sounded like hate, people had to agree that his political and social views were correct. Malcolm was a master debater, and most people would not dare to challenge him, including King. When Malcolm and Rustin had a debate at Howard University, Malcolm destroyed Rustin, so Farmer was determined not to let that happen to him. Malcolm and Farmer had a debate at Cornell University in 1962. Farmer opened the debate by asking Malcolm to give a program or plan for the salvation of black people. Malcolm answered by quoting Elijah Muhammad's calling for land or a black state or demanding that the government return money owed to blacks for reparations and to purchase an island somewhere in the globe where they could live.

Farmer knew that this was Malcolm's weakest area because Malcolm had to echo Elijah Muhammad and not speak his own mind. When Malcolm approached the platform, for two or three minutes, he talked about how much he respected Farmer because he was the only top leader of so-called Negroes who had guts to face him in a public debate. Farmer knew Malcolm was fishing for something to say because this was Malcolm's weakest area. Malcolm finally replied without attacking Farmer, but he attacked the idiocy of nonviolence by saying:

> Someone slaps you on one cheek and you're going to turn the other? What kind of sense is that? You've seen it on TV! You've seen those fire hose rolling black women down the streets! The skirt's flying! You've seen the police dogs turned loose on little black children, biting their flesh and tearing their

clothes! And then he roared, "Don't let those dogs bite those children! Kill the damn dogs!"[30]

The crowd went wild.

In 1963, Malcolm's prominence in the media and the black community caused envy between him and the Nation of Islam officials. The Nation of Islam officials had started up businesses within the community, profiting greatly from those enterprises. They had land, a jet plane, and many houses. Many ministers had never earned this amount money before, and they knew that they were spending money in ways that Malcolm did not want them to spend. And they knew that Malcolm was next in line to oversee the Nation of Islam.

Elijah Muhammad was very ill at the time. In fact, in an attempt to undermine Malcolm, these men elaborated charges against him and convinced Elijah Muhammad that he was trying to take over the Nation of Islam and denounce his name. So Elijah suspended Malcolm ninety days for making comments about John F. Kennedy's death. Despite being disciplined, Malcolm's spirituality allowed him to remain humble toward Elijah until he realized that Elijah would never reinstate him back to his rank. But Malcolm always credited Elijah for raising him up from the dead, giving him back his sight, and causing him to think for himself.

> I, myself, being one who was lost and dead, buried here in the rubbish of the West in the thickest darkness of sin and ignorance (hoodwinked by the false teachings of the Slavemaster) am able to stand upright today, perpendicular, on the square with my God (Allah) and my own kind… able for the first time in 400 years to

see and hear…I bear witness that Messenger Elijah Muhammad has been taught (raised) by this Great God Allah, and today…is…teaching us and raising us from the ignorant dead.[31]

Malcolm's religious commitment was determined by his will to serve Allah and not Elijah Muhammad. Elijah Muhammad was compared to Moses and the other prophets in the Bible. The Nation of Islam officials parallel Elijah to Moses and Malcolm to Aaron. For instance, Elijah was compared with Moses, who spoke for God, and Malcolm was identified with Aaron, who spoke for Moses. This belief is still true today.

As a black Muslim, Malcolm believed in the doctrine of doom to white America. According to this doctrine, white America was based on (1) the black Muslim myth of Yacob; (2) the biblical theme of justice and judgement, especially in the prophets and the Revelation of John; and (3) historical observation.[32] The Yacob myth claimed that an evil black scientist created the devil white race six thousand years ago. According to Malcolm, justice meant that God will destroy America for her sins. Malcolm thought that history repeats itself. Just as Noah warned the people of his time about the coming of flood and Lot warned the Sodomites of the coming fire, God raised up Elijah Muhammad to warn white America of its coming destruction. The black Muslims today believe that we are still living in the time predicted by the old prophets of God. I disagree with the theology that whites are devils; however, I feel that everyone should be aware of other theologies.

While Martin's theology focused on love and forgiveness, and he hoped that blacks and whites could create the beloved community, Malcolm's ideology stressed strict justice and harsh punishment, and he hoped that God would destroy the entire white race and then establish a world of peace and goodwill among all blacks. In addition, Malcolm stressed justice for blacks by any means necessary, while Martin emphasized justice for blacks through love for whites. Also, Martin developed the nonviolent philosophy, while Malcolm declared his commitment to self-defense. Furthermore, Malcolm despised Martin's turn the other cheek philosophy, and he insisted that blacks should use the eye-for-eye philosophy because that's the only language the white oppressors understood.

Even though Martin is associated with a deep religious commitment, a case could be made that Malcolm was more religious than Martin if we evaluated the terms of their obedience to the moral code of their religion. For instance, Martin acknowledged that he preached a morality that he sometimes violated, while Malcolm faithfully obeyed the strict moral code of the Black Muslim religion. While there were rumors about Martin's adulterous affairs, Malcolm continued to refrain from smoking, drinking, fornication, and adultery, and eating pork and corn bread. However, I believe that these men should not be judged by professed moral codes, but they should be judged by their deeds and commitment to freedom, justice, and equality for humanity because everyone has sinned and fallen short of glory.

Despite the public's view of the differences between these two men, they had similarities as well. Theologically, they both appealed to the Bible as a major source for their claims. For example, they often referred to Moses, Daniel,

Paul, Lazarus, and Jesus. They both preached about the lost sheep, the wheat and the tares, the prodigal son, and the great Exodus. They were both sons of black Baptist preachers. Malcolm's father was Earl Little, and he was an advocate of Malcolm Garvey. King was the son of Martin, Sr., who was the pastor of Ebenezer Baptist Church in Atlanta. Both men were ministers, just like their fathers. Also, they both were changed by their contact with religious ideas outside of America. For Malcolm, the inspiration emerged from his trip to Mecca, and for King it was India. In addition, Malcolm became King when he went to Mecca, and King became Malcolm when went to live in Chicago. They both realized that racism transcended race, gender, and religion. Consequently, both men faced constant death threats, bombed houses, and enemies on every hand, and they knew that they would not live long lives.

King is credited for being the greatest civil rights leaders in this century. But if a person really studies the life of King, he or she would realize that King was more than a civil rights leader for oppressed people. King was a man that really tried to follow the Christian doctrine of reconciliation as it applied to race and the ministry of Jesus Christ. This is how he was able to remain nonviolent when he could have turned to violence. This doctrine gave meaning and purpose to the nonviolent philosophy that established the civil rights movement. For King, being a Christian meant being totally committed to the love ethic of Jesus. The scriptures were the inspiration behind King's theology and thinking. King believed that the choice for Negroes or white Americans was not between violence and nonviolence; the choice was between nonviolence and nonexistence.

King argued and believed that nonviolence was the means to create a black community characterized by positiveness and unity. The method of reconciliation brings together people from different backgrounds. Also, reconciliation helps to create the beloved community, which is only possible through love and nonviolence. This is what King believed in and died for. This is how he could quote the Bible, saying that "God so loved the world" that through the person of Jesus Christ the brokenness was restored by act of redemption, which took place on the cross at cavalry. King preached what he practiced and practiced what he preached. For instance, his life indicated that a person must work within the struggle to relate the Christian faith to the condition that affects the body and soul; an individual must believe in reconciliation, and a person must be willing to lay down his or her life in the quest for freedom, justice, and equality. Also, a person must have faith. And for him it was faith in the gospel of Jesus that related to suffering and heavy burden. This is how he remained hopeful in hopeless situations.

Malcolm's leaving the Nation of Islam enabled him to cooperate with other civil rights leaders, including King. Malcolm's organization, "Organization of Afro-American Unity," was developed to work with any group that was interested in dealing with problems of injustice, racism, and oppression. Before his split with the Nation of Islam, his religious beliefs were made public, but under the order of Elijah Muhammad he had to keep his political statements silent. That impeded him from being involved in the political process and the civil rights movement. For example, under Elijah Muhammad's leadership, the Nation of Islam did not believe in going to the polls and voting. But after his break with the NOI, this situation was reversed. Malcolm assigned religion to the private arena and placed politics in the center of his public dialogue. The new Malcolm discontinued his critique of the black church in the interest of unity and explicated the politics of Black Nationalism. He even stated that if people visited a church and that church brought black people together, then people should join that church. He said the same thing about civil rights organizations. Unity in the black community was Malcolm's central theme after he left the Nation of Islam because he was free to do the will of Allah. Elijah Muhammad had dominance over Malcolm's political opinions and beliefs. As a black Muslim, Malcolm was not permitted to think for himself, but only for Elijah Muhammad. Malcolm's trip to Egypt, Lebanon, Saudi Arabia, Nigeria, Ghana, Morocco, and Algeria made an enormous impact upon his understanding of Islam and his perspective on Black Nationalism. In Mecca, he discovered that Elijah Muhammad's Islamic teachings contradicted orthodox Islam. Malcolm saw white Muslims in Mecca treating persons of other races, including himself, as brothers and sisters; they were not showing prejudice or disrespect whatsoever. This experience changed his whole theology.

Although Malcolm spoke of his spiritual rebirth, his early images of preaching so-called violence persuaded a lot people to stay away from him. This conduct really hurt the movement, as well as Malcolm's potential to lead the masses to greater heights. This rebirth broadened his spectrum, but it did not keep him from speaking his mind. He believed that he could relate to whites who were trying to identify with him. However, one would never see him trying to get along with whites who opposed him. Malcolm's conversion gave him new thoughts about integration and intermarriages, as observed in his following statement:

> I believe in recognizing every human being as a human being, neither white, black, brown nor red. When you are dealing with humanity as one family, there's no question of integration or intermarriage. It's just one human being marrying another human being, or one human being living around and with another human being. I may say, though, that I don't think the burden to defend any such position should ever be upon the black man. Because it is the white man collectively who has shown that he is hostile toward integration and toward intermarriages and toward these other strides toward oneness.[33]

Malcolm's spirituality allowed him to search for truth and walk by faith. After his split with Elijah, he did not have the economical support he had before; therefore, he did not know where his future was heading or which direction he was going. But he was certain that he was for freedom by any means necessary. No one in the century stated his/her opinion more bluntly than Malcolm. His spirituality allowed him to say things that most blacks wanted to say, but they were afraid to say them. For instance, he labeled this era an "Era of Hypocrisy."

King and Malcolm's spirituality allowed both men to speak the truth to the ruling power structures on behalf of oppressed, powerless, and voiceless peoples. Both men believed that freedom was not free and death was the price that an individual had to pay. Both men were exposed to ideas of liberation and freedom for humankind since birth. Their lives signified that there could be no understanding of the gospel apart from God's unity with the liberation struggles of the poor, because the freedom of the victims on earth is the hope of God's intention to redeem the whole human creation. This was why they could go to church and preach: "The Spirit of the Lord is upon me, because he has anointed me to preach the gospel to the poor; he hath sent me to heal the brokenhearted, to preach deliverance to the captives, and recovering of sight to the blind, to set at liberty them that are bruised. To preach the acceptable year of he Lord."[34]

King and Malcolm both represented the good Samaritan and not the priest and the Levite. They stopped and helped a sick nation to change from her prejudiced ways by speaking out and giving biblical and economical solutions to the racial problems in America. Even though they paid the "innkeeper" by different means, one with Visa, the other with MasterCard. Nevertheless, we cannot take away the fact that their commitment to their God and their religious beliefs helped America become the nation it is today. Both men allowed their spirituality to articulate their dreams and nightmares with a passion that no one else would be able to surpass.

As one tries to do the will of God and speak on behalf of the powerless, one cannot help but to notice that the dream and nightmare are still alive. For instance, the dream is alive because black children and white children are holding hands and playing together, they are sitting in classrooms together, and white people and black people are working side by side in factories and industrial plants. The nightmare is still a reality because the masses of black people are still living in poverty, and/or on drugs; prostitution is still alive, and racism is alive and well in this society. Furthermore, one should commend Malcolm for speaking the truth and conveying the importance of black history. He also underscored the importance of loving oneself as well as one's blackness. In addition, one should also be grateful to King for helping blacks to understand that love transcends hate; and this should be a central message as one follows Christ.

The Million Man March of October 16, 1995 was an unforgettable day that will go down in history as one of the most inspirational events recorded for black men. This day was truly consecrated by God. Who could have inspired and propitiated the gathering of over one million black men in an atmosphere of peace and clarity, without violence erupting or confusion occurring? No one on this earth could have done so. This was an act of divine intercession. Yes, the call came through Louis Farrakhan, but the call was given by God. No one in this lifetime who lives in this society ever thought that one million black men would come together to talk about becoming better men for the sake of their communities, women, and children; getting closer to God; and manhood and brotherhood. Also, men went to the march for other reasons. Some went to atone for their behaviors because atonement is a spiritual concept that indicates a conscious intent to seek redemption. Some went to unite with their long and lost brothers. Some men went to forgive because forgiveness appeals to the heart and it helps to release anger and make ways for change. Some men went to heal because healing indicates that an individual recognizes that something is wrong. Whatever reasons black men went for, no one can take from them the dignity and integrity of that march because the spirit of the God was felt there. Many said they had never been in a place like that where there was so much love, affection, adoration, fondness, passion, appreciation, attachment, and trust expressed between black men.

Critics have said that nothing good has come out of the march because the results have been inconclusive; however, most men went to the march not to be seen, but to make inner changes. African Americans wanted to work within themselves before trying to work with others. In fact, most of the black men who were there went to see how they could rebuild themselves individually first, and then collectively. African Americans have lived under the rules of white supremacy for almost four hundred years now. This has caused blacks to be divided, angry, and fragmented. It is lamentable that the results of the march are not going to be seen collectively and visually anytime soon. Besides, the group was not together long enough to produce any public changes. How can one day of unity between black men compete with four hundred years of a system that is rooted and designed in white supremacy? But one thing positive was proven true during the march: there is really strength in numbers, and reconciliation restores trust.

The Million Man March was faced with opposing struggles—victory and frustration, joy and pain, and pride and shame—but through it all this was the day that the Lord had made. When Ted Koppel concluded his TV coverage on the Million Man March on *Nightline*, he stated that the Million Man March was the largest, most peaceful mass assembly in the history of Washington Mall. It was the most calm, prayerful, joyful, loving, spirit-filled march that I have ever participated in, even though the media and some black preachers, teachers, politicians, and other leaders were against the march because the call came through Farrakhan, it did not stop brave men, women, and children from participating. Many leaders and top officials have problems with Farrakhan and his message. But as long as racism exists in this country and other countries, African Americans should listen to anyone who has the boldness to address these issues of segregation, race reconciliation, and positive race interactions.

In addition, many black leaders really wanted to attend, but they were advised by their superiors that it would be in their best interest if they did not go. Some African Americans were instructed by their pastors not to go because Farrakhan was a major figure of the march. Several Christians stated that they did not serve Farrakhan, but Jesus. In fact, Bishop Eddie Long of New Birth Full Gospel Baptist Church in Decatur, Georgia stated that anybody who goes to MMM is anti-Christ. I was offended, because he is thinking for me. I think for myself. That is why I am free. This type of plantation theology generated a lot of confusion within the black community. The truth of the matter is if someone's house is on fire, s/he will not care about who helps to put it out—help will be accepted regardless of who offers it. The black community is on fire in America, and help is needed to extinguish this inferno. We need solutions that address economics, poverty, drugs, crime, violence, AIDS, and other issues that are prevalent in the black community. African Americans should be open and listen to anyone who affirms that they have solutions to the plight of black Americans.

The Million Man March reminds one of the biblical stories of Gideon pulling down the altar of Baal. In the Book of Judges 6: 25–30, God had called Gideon to be Israel's savior and commanded Gideon to tear down the altar of Baal, which was a pagan god. This charge really tested Gideon's faith because Gideon would be putting his life on the line. However, Gideon went at night and pulled down the altar of Baal. When the townspeople discovered that Baal had been torn down, they wanted to kill the person or persons who did it. Moreover, it was recognized that Gideon had done this, and the townspeople wanted to kill him. These people were of the same race. However, instead of them turning on the ones that were oppressing them, they turned on Gideon, who was on their side.

This story is identical to that of the Million Man March. When Farrakhan first announced the call of the MMM, many Negroes turned against Farrakhan rather than turning against the sin and racism. The only thing Farrakhan did was to pull down the altar of Baal. White supremacy is an altar of Baal. This is why the media portrayed Farrakhan as a symbol of hate; because he is not afraid to speak the truth regarding racism. Farrakhan is one of the few leaders in this country that can get on television and speak harshly to the white power structures of this country. The reason he can do this is that he does not depend on whites economically. I understand that Farrakhan is not an enemy to black peoples but to whites because he views them as being devils. I disagree. This is his weakness. He could be much more effective if he preached reconciliation instead of separation. This type of theology must change. This is why America needs racial reconciliation. This country was built upon racism. Racism is a system that denies human beings their rights, jobs, and opportunities. Racism is a demonic separatist ideology that goes against the teaching of Jesus Christ, who commanded that his followers love one another. Racism is not a Christian-based theology. The dominant orders of this society perpetuate racism and maintain power for themselves and their children. As a matter of fact, Abraham Lincoln stated that "If I could keep slavery and preserve the Union, then I would. Because I as any other white man want the position of superiority assigned to the white race, and the position of inferiority assigned to the black race."[35] This type of indoctrination has been passed down from generation to generation. Since white supremacy is a major concern of black people and white leaders alike, then all involved should listen to Farrakhan's economic and political solutions, which call for shared power and opportunity regardless of race.

In light of the historical injustices that have victimized blacks in this society, one should wonder why these same oppressed people would turn on each other, kill and cheat each other rather than direct their resentment toward racism. I wonder why African Americans always believe everything whites say. Why do so many African Americans give up and sell out, turning his/her back on the poor and downtrodden in the African American community. After everything the African race has gone through in the United States, just to receive the right to vote, it appears that they should be willing to do anything that would help the struggle for total emancipation. In addition, the struggle is not going to be easy. Blacks must become more enterprising. Frederick Douglass said, "If there is no struggle, there is no progress. Those who profess to favor freedom, and yet depreciate agitation, are men who want crops without plowing up the ground. They want rain without thunder and lighting…This struggle may be a moral and physical; but there must be a struggle."[36]

Racism is evil, but what was meant for bad turned out good because slavery brought America adversity and adversity builds character. Racism should motivate African Americans to learn to think for themselves and to pool their resources together to create jobs and businesses. They should also invest in the black community so that it will no longer be controlled by those who advocate racism. When Farrakhan, Jesse Jackson, and other prominent black leaders first began to talk about the Million Man March, the first thing the media and the government did was try to stop the march by using at least three tactics. First, they spread fear in the country, painting a picture of violence that several people thought would break out. Second was distrust. Here, they implied there would be corruption in the handling of funds associated with the march. They raised questions like, "Where is the money going?" and, "Who is getting it?" Third was envy. They insinuated that Farrakhan was an unfit leader, and asking questions like: "Why or how is it that Farrakhan has become the head of the black community?" Many organized efforts from racist segments of this society attempted to stop the Million Man March, but God blessed the participants and there was nothing they could do but become spectators and listen to the speakers, which included males and females, including Rosa Parks. The following is the pledge of the MMM which African Americans should adapt in order to better relations within and outside the community:

> I pledge that from this day forward I will strive to love my brother as I love myself, I from this day forward, will to improve myself spiritually, morally, mentally, socially, politically, and economically for the benefit of myself, my family, and my people. I pledge that I will strive to build businesses, build houses, build hospitals, build factories, and enter into international trade for good of myself, my family, and my people. I pledge that from this day forward I will never raise my hand with a knife or a gun to beat, cut, shoot any member of my family or any human being except in self-defense. I pledge from this day forward I will never abuse my wife by striking her or disrespecting her, for she is the mother of my children and the producer of my future. I pledge that from this day forward I will never engage in the abuse of children, little boys or little girls, for sexual gratification. For I will let them grow in peace to be strong men and women for the future of our people. I will never again use the B-word to describe any female—but particularly my own black sister. I pledge from this day forward that I will not poison my body with drugs or that which is destructive to my health and my well-being. I pledge from this day forward I will support Black newspapers, Black radio, and Black television. I will support Black artists who clean up their act to show respect for their people and respect for the heirs of the human family. I will do all of this, so help me God.[37]

What is wrong with this pledge? What is wrong with gangsters changing from bad to good? The Million Man March continues to be one the major event in contemporary African American history. It inspired millions throughout the country and the world. People of all kinds came to answer the call of God. In the words of Cornell West and others, "Long live the spirit of the Million Man March."

Chapter 3

> Injustice anywhere is threat to justice everywhere.
> —Martin L. King Jr.

From the moment *Do The Right Thing* opened, Spike Lee's movie has raised many questions and has caused controversy and disagreements among critics and moviegoers. This movie addresses complex issues such as racial discrimination, prejudice, capitalism, and poverty. For instance, the core of the movie ends with Sal and his sons closing the doors for the night. However, youngsters from the neighborhood gather at the door, asking for one more piece of pizza. Sal, the Italian owner, who is feeling compassionate after a profitable day, decides to give in to their request. At this moment, a character named Buggin Out, who is organizing a boycott against Sal because Sal does not have any black heroes on the wall, walks in with Radio Raheem and Smiley. Earlier in the movie, there were arguments between Smiley and Sal's prejudiced son, Pino, and Sal and Radio Raheem. Meanwhile, Smiley shakes his pictures of Martin and Malcolm, while Raheem turns his radio up to full volume.

After a long and hot day and having to scream to be heard, Sal loses control, calls Raheem a nigger, grabs a baseball bat, and demolishes Raheem's radio. In retaliation, Raheem attacks Sal. He, in turn, is attacked by Sal's sons. Buggin Out and Smiley join in and the confrontation carries onto the sidewalk. The crowd gathers, the police arrive, and as violence and chaos increase, the cops put a choke hold on Radio Raheem to restrain him. Instead, they kill him. After the cops leave from the scene, Mookie throws a garbage can into Sal's window and Sal's establishment is looted and burned down. However, Lee does not end the movie with hatred, frustration, and destruction. Rather, he ends it with an uneasy, iffy rapprochement between Sal and Mookie the next morning.

Spike Lee is considered to be a political radical because his movies deal with issues confronting blacks and other minorities. He also explores negative images that exist in this society. One message in this movie has been compared to the first chapter of *The Souls of Black Folk* by W. E. B. Du Bois, in which the author describes the African American consciousness as a basic "two-ness, double-consciousness...two souls, two thoughts, two unreconciled striving; two warring ideals in one dark body." Throughout *Do the Right Thing,* Mookie is faced with this very consciousness. From Buggin Out, he hears, "Stay black;" from Mother Sister, "Don't work too hard today;" from Jade, "Take care of your responsibilities;" from his wife, Tina, "Be a man;" from Sal, "You're f-ckin up;" and from Da Mayor, "Always try to do the right thing." Other perceptions regarding this double consciousness can be seen between Sal and Buggin Out, Pina and Vito, Da Mayor and Mother Sister, Jade and Tina, whiteness and blackness, King and X, cool and hot, love and hate, right thing and wrong thing, and violence and nonviolence. Thanks to Mookie, these messages and images help blacks to question themselves by wondering what the top priority in the black community is. Is it investing or supporting this community, or is it supporting yourself and your family? The message of the love/hate lesson from Radio Raheem was a positive one. He explains that

> The Right-Hand-Left-Hand, the tale of Good and Evil… The story of Life is this: Static! One hand is always fighting the other. Left Hand Hate is kicking much ass and it looks like Right Hand Love is finished. Hold up. Stop the presses! The Right Hand is coming back! Yes, it's love. Love has won. Left Hand Hate KO'ed by Love.

In the end, Radio Raheem was killed by the very hate his character challenges.

The movie underscores the fact that in this society whites; blacks; rich; poor; democrats; republicans; white politicians; young, black rappers; conservatives; and liberals are always fighting against one another. Pino, who is a racist, called blacks niggers and coons all the time. However, when Mookie asks him who his favorite basketball player was, he stated Magic Johnson; his favorite movie star, Eddie Murphy; his favorite rock star, he uttered Prince. This dualism is a moral issue that should also be considered. Why do blacks and whites think differently?

The pictures of King and Malcolm were particularly effective in displaying the power that blacks have as a people if individual differences could be put aside in favor of unity within the race. King and Malcolm X forced this country to deal with the racial problem existing in America. If blacks and whites came together as a body and pooled their resources, as Public Enemy says, "a nation of millions couldn't hold us back," and America would be a better place. Both King and Malcolm represented "freedom" and "unity" and other positive images and messages in their speeches and in their life.

As one analyzes *Do the Right Thing*, one must admit that it was rather mesmerizing. The plot contained nudity, positive messages, and violence. However, one question that could be raised refers to what Spike Lee meant to convey to his audience when his character said that the Koreans were okay. How does Lee come to this conclusion? Lee points out earlier in the movie that the Koreans talk about us too and that they were just as manipulative as Sal was. This part of the movie could be viewed as a contradiction. How could the looters all of sudden become so loving toward the Koreans? Sal did not kill Raheem; the cops did. Just as Sal was making money and taking it to another part of the town, the Koreans were doing the same thing. In reality, the Koreans did not even have a black employee. Sal had a black person on the payroll. He also told Mookie that there would always be a place for him. Mookie never touched the money, but he had his freedom and he was not imprisoned or on the street robbing and killing. Smiley was showing the picture of Martin and Malcolm all during the movie as to represent unity among black people or unite every race and religion. The looters would have burned down the Koreans' store as well, given that they were not considered part of the black family. Furthermore, since the crowd burned down Sal's establishment, then it appears that it also should burn down the Korean store, thus making the movie more realistic. When people riot they burn everything in sight. Besides, most of Lee's films do not conclude with happy endings. This is what makes Spike Lee the formidable filmmaker that he is.

Do the Right Thing accomplished its purposes by addressing the racial problems in America and raising questions in the audience's mind such as, "What are Sal and Mookie going to do now? Will the cops be charged with police brutality? Did Mookie 'do the right thing?' Whose political philosophy was right? Martin L. King Jr's or Malcolm X's?" Who should we follow today? Jesse Jackson, Louis Farrakhan, Rush Limbaugh, Ann Coulter, or President Obama? The audience is forced to create its own ending. The movie's perception of the racial problem in America is an accurate one. Racism is still prevalent today, and its manifestation is getting stronger. The movie does convey the message that black people need to wake up.

Finally, this film is also positive because it represents truth. It is educational. It is unique because of its positive messages and lack of drive-by shootings or helicopters flying around to represent war. There was also love and unity, represented in the moment the community came together to fight back in response to Raheem's death. Moreover, this movie was entertaining and gave the positive lesson that one should "Always Do The Right Thing." The pictures of Martin and Malcolm represent unity among black people with different beliefs. Despite Martin and Malcolm's beliefs, they fought the same injustices. The lesson that we should learn from their lives is that we must work together to fight discrimination.

Lethal Weapon 4 is about two cops; one is black, and one is white. Together, they are fighting an Asian mob that is smuggling Chinese immigrants to America and selling them as slaves. Danny Glover, who is a black cop, father, and husband, accidentally discovers a boatload of slaves and takes them to his home. This reason for taking them into his house is that he can relate to them as being slaves. Mel Gibson, a white cop who is single and living with his girlfriend, detects the Chinese immigrants living in Glover's house. Eventually, the Chinese gangsters find out that the slaves are staying with the Glovers, so they take the slaves and burn down the Glovers' house. This is how the other characters come in the scene.

For instance, Jet Li, who plays the villain, is a ruthless gangster who smuggles Chinese laborers into this country and sells them into slavery. Rene Russo plays Mel Gibson's girlfriend. Chris Rock plays a young detective who has gotten Danny Glover's daughter pregnant. Joe Pesci plays an annoying private investigator who is a joke or a clown. Together, Gibson, Glover, Russo, Rock, and Pesci take on the Chinese syndicate, eventually break up the slave trade operation and freeing the immigrants. In the end, they claim that they are not friends but they are a family. This film was full of action and appears to have pleased the audience. However, there were messages in this film that were unclear. For example, what was the message of a maniac who is standing in the middle of Los Angeles spraying shots and throwing flames?

In addition, the racial image of this movie consistently reflects Hollywood's image that white is superior and black is inferior. For instance, Mel Gibson, who is white, is the leader, a step ahead of everyone else, and he is a thinker. On the other hand, blacks play secondary roles. For instance, during the beginning of the film, while the man in the mask and body armor is spraying up Los Angeles, Mel Gibson immediately tells Danny Glover to strip and flap his arms like a wild chicken, and Glover does it. How does Hollywood come up with this type of script for black characters? Why couldn't the writers reverse the script and let Danny Glover tell Mel Gibson to flap his wings? Does perpetuating stereotypes that blacks are inhuman and unintelligent "play a role" here? Also, Chris Rock is characterized as a young cop who grew up in a "bad neighborhood." Why could he not have come from an honorable, middle class family?

Moreover, Danny Glover thought Rock was gay because Rock was being extra nice to him. Why could he not portray a black man who was sensible and kind without sounding less masculine? Later on in the film, the true reason was revealed why Chris Rock was being extra nice to Glover; he had impregnated Glover's daughter. Evidence has proven that Hollywood's images still portray black actors and actresses as modern Coons, Mulatta, Mammies, and Bucks because scripts geared toward black characters are censored and in most cases are written by whites. Therefore, Negroes are not and cannot be themselves. They are still subjects in a discourse of white protagonists. Whenever a Negro signs his/her name on the dotted line to work for Hollywood, he/she has to act the way Hollywood wants him or her to act. And in most cases

Hollywood wants black actors and actresses to play characters who are full of folly. This is why Chris Rock was brought into this film; he is a famous comedian who will say or do anything to get a laugh. The roles Gibson, Russo, Pesçi, and Li played were serious roles, but Glover and Rock, who are black, have had the roles of comedians or pranksters.

Furthermore, Hollywood still dramatizes white women to be purely passionate, genuine, and gutsy. This is how Rene Russo has scored big in her role. Several critics have stated that she is the next best thing in the movie other than Jet Li. Russo's image portrayed her as being a super woman who will stand up and fight the Chinese gangsters even though she is pregnant, and she even wins the fight. This is how Hollywood gives the message abroad that white Americans, whether males or females, are brave, courageous, and fearless. Another image that parallels this one is that of the Pontiac versus the Mercedes, which implies that America's products are better than foreign ones.

Another stereotypical image portrayed in this movie is that most Chinese people are karate experts. Whenever an Asian male is in a Hollywood film, he is a martial arts expert. Also, Asians are portrayed as being very serious. It seems that people of every race are considered intense thinkers except African Americans. Hollywood shows no interest in portraying African Americans as intelligent human beings; they are consistently described as an inferior race. These kinds of intentional misleading images and messages are negatives and disruptive to racial reconciliation and harmony. It is also pejorative in that it persistently inculcates inferiority complexes in the minds of African Americans—one reason why many blacks do not go to movies that aim to please white audiences. This film was action-packed and had lots of "make-believe" stunts that white audiences really enjoy. For example, Mel Gibson, the leading character, rides down the Los Angeles freeway on a table that fell off of a truck after he had just beaten an Asian karate expert. The Asian gets killed, but Mel Gibson survives. Once again, according to Hollywood's standard, white is superior and other races are inferior.

As stated, Hollywood dramatizes that all Chinese citizens are martial arts experts, all white men are leaders and thinkers, and all blacks are marginal and buffoons. This is giving false images and messages to audiences everywhere. This film could have been a good one if the writers, producers, and directors had had more realistic images and messages. For example, Chris Rock's and Danny Glover's characters should have been more serious than they were. Furthermore, Glover's wife should have been the one fighting the Chinese gangsters instead of a pregnant woman since the modem slaves had been place in her house first.

One other unpleasant aspect of this movie is its humor. For instance, there were lots of jokes that were directed at Chinese people. In conclusion, this film also exploits the claim that America is a land of democracy. Notice in last scene of the movie the captain informs Glover that the immigrants will be able to remain in America and become citizens of the United States. This is how America is being portrayed as a cup of tea, but once they come they see a different side of this nation: the reality. They see that this is an unequal and racist society. This film is too violent, it has derogatory images, and it is not entertaining.

Chapter 4

A Model for Racial Reconciliation

> Life's most persistent and urgent question is, What are you doing for others?
> —Martin L. King Jr.

Howard Thurman was one of the spiritual fathers of this nation's struggle for racial justice. His contribution to the civil rights movement was a spiritual one. From his pulpit, he advocated equality of all peoples and underscored the importance of harmonious living within the races. Thurman was a prolific writer and poet, a respected scholar, and an influential theologian who emphasized interdenominational spirituality and love. He died in 1981 but left a significant legacy of racial harmony that has inspired the model adopted by the writer of this dissertation.

The same concern toward racial reconciliation within the church and the community displayed by Thurman in the 1940s can observed in the theology of Curtiss Paul DeYoung, who questions the authenticity and validity of the current rhetoric surrounding racial reconciliation, saying that while it sounds positive, in actuality, it's not as DeYoung states:

> Our world is ripping at the seams because of hatred, violence, racism, classism, sexism, homophobia, nationalism, and anti-Semitism. Events like ethnic cleaning and urban street battles seem diametrically opposed to the forces of reconciliation, as do continuing problems like the domination of women and the corporate exploitation of the poor.[38]

Concern for social, racial, and economical justice was also at the center of Howard Thurman's theology, particularly when he cofounded the Church for the Fellowship of All Peoples in San Francisco, California in 1944. This effort was pioneering in promoting unity and oneness through an interfaith fellowship and fostering coherence between the theoretical racial reconciliation discourse and the intervention of the church to alleviate the racial, social, and economic divide that DeYoung talks about in the previous statement. Thurman was convinced that "a way could be found to create a religious fellowship worthy of transcending racial, cultural, and social distinctions."[39] His church had an interdenominational membership as well as a diverse, cross-cultural body. Other members were "humanists with widest range of political concerns and orientation."[40] In this context, intercultural and international activities were carried out consistently. The members of this church had a common objective, which was "hunger for a better way of living together,"[41] one that only God could inspire and realize.

The following formed the basis for membership in the Church for the Fellowship of All Peoples: 1) need for a growing understanding of all men as sons of God; 2) seeking a vital experience of God as revealed in Jesus of Nazareth; 3) spiritual interaction with other great religious spirits whose fellowship with God was the foundation of their fellowship with man; 4) desire to grow spiritually and to have an ethical awareness of men and women of varied national, cultural, racial, and creedal heritage united in a religious fellowship.[42]

Thurman's new church eliminated its Calvinist makeup so as to give the new congregation the "freedom to open wide its door to all denominations, nationalities, races, and cultures who desired to live their daily lives by the tenets of such a demanding commitment."[43] In this congregation, Thurman put his major theological concern to a great test. In doing so, he raised the question, Is the centrality and significance of worshiping the Lord foremost in human life? In his view, when in the presence of God humans are simply humans; any other arbitrary categorization insofar as gender, age, class, or political affiliation ceases to have validity. It matters not who one is, but rather if one worships God sincerely.

Members of this religious body found strength in the reconciliatory spiritual infrastructure of the church. They felt empowered by it to deal with and to reconcile social and racial issues within their community and, consequently, their nation.

As Thurman stated, "increasing numbers of people who were engaged in the common life of the city of San Francisco found in the church restoration, inspiration, and courage for their work on behalf of social change in the community."[44] The church assumed a catalyst role in promoting restoration and unity for a diverse group of believers. Its worship hour became, as Thurman puts it, a "watering hole"[45] for all peoples. The Christlike "water" found in this spiritual oasis replenished and nurtured the human spirit. Consequently, it inspired the membership to reach out to the community and to bridge the racial divide prevalent in that perfidiously prejudicial era. The church's religious commitment concerned (1) the spirit, (2) the worshipping of God, and (3) the community.

Thurman also participated in community events in an attempt to tangibly share the love of God with all peoples. Love taught Thurman understanding and acceptance of others. This allowed him to eventually "find ultimate security in an ultimate vulnerability."[46] Love enabled Thurman to accomplish much. He was able to understand and to communicate with others in order to foster a feeling of belonging in an environment traditionally hostile to nonwhites.

Also, the Fellowship Church was a testing ground for Thurman's model for racial and spiritual unity. To empower his congregation toward achieving a pragmatic theology of unity and inclusiveness, he had to reevaluate traditional values such as goodwill, which he regarded as "futile sentimentality."[47] To strengthen the love as well as the spiritual and fraternal bonds within the congregation, Thurman planned outings where members would interact in settings like restaurants and social halls to have intercultural fellowship dinners. These events were planned by different racial groups within the church.

Thurman also added a library to this congregation, which served as historic depository for the various cultural and racial groups of the fellowship. The library was also used to chronicle the progress being achieved by the group in its effort to truly worship God in unity of spirit and experience. He derived initial support for this effort from royalties received from his first book.

In his effort to promote unity through fellowship, Thurman also created a Sunday Coffee Hour, which proved to be of great importance in deepening the member's understanding of each other. He also organized intercultural workshops for children to pass on to them the richness and diversity of the cultures represented within the church and in the world. By sensitizing and informing the children in this way, Thurman was assuring that his efforts toward reconciliation and spiritual unity would be carried on into the future and not become just a legacy of a failed ideology. As he describes it in one particular summer:

> Hopi Indian children from Arizona were invited to visit us as guest of the children's intercultural workshop. It was very illuminating for these children to discover that they recognized many of the games and exercises the other ethnic group shared in common. Included in such orientation was an introduction to the great religion as well. One small boy who had made a great discovery told his mother when he went home, "I knew Jesus was a Baptist, but I had no idea he was a Jew!"[48]

Fellowship such as the one described above broadened the member's views of fellowship to include interaction with others. In the extended vision, members would also interact with fellow workers, business associates, etc. This philosophy of inclusion became known as contact with fellowship, which was a true exercise of meaningful goodwill. Such unity and spirituality existing in a time and context of bitter conflict, as seen in World War II, was quite revolutionary and unprecedented. While the United States and allied forces were trying to secure liberation for a world held by fascist, racist, ideals, Thurman was doing all he could to assure that his church, his community, and ultimately his country, could become a model for racial and cultural integration through the worship of God—the only one who could transform and unite humankind with his love.

Thurman remained optimistic about the continuation of his ideals for unrestricted human interaction and acceptance. He believed that "any barrier that separated one person from another can be undermined and eliminated."[49] He explored other facets of spiritual involvement by also incorporating liturgical dance during the worship. He eventually encouraged the formation of a dance choir, an English handbell choir, and a musical choir. He also motivated these worship groups to reach out to the community and to perform in hospitals and wherever destitute and spiritually needy persons could be found. The church's choir even performed at the "4th Plenary session of UNESCO, in Paris, travelling under the auspices of the church's intercultural worshop."[50]

Membership in the church increased rapidly and proved that Thurman's theology of inclusion was also sound from a humanistic point of view, even when put to a test. He experienced rejection and prejudice as he visited members in hospitals or in other settings, but in every situation he stood firm in his faith and convictions, powerfully witnessing his gospel of acceptance and unity. Consequently, he would always be respected in the end for it. In many instances, the very persons who discriminated against him or his members would have a change of heart and eventually even visit and/or join his church. Thurman lived his life affirming his concept of community, unity of the races, and of unified worship. He also extended his spirit of fellowship through speaking engagements and membership in associations like the YWCA, the Conference of Christians and Jews, the Urban League, the NAACP, the International Institute, the Mental Health Council, and the Council for Civic Unity, the Commonwealth Club, the San Francisco Symphony Orchestra, and the San Francisco Choral Society. Thurman also presented his message of oneness in spirit and in life for all peoples in commencement speeches, Jewish temples, etc.

The Church for the Fellowship of all Peoples also contributed to the dissemination and the spread of black history and culture, thus pioneering the significance of black identity and consciousness.

The church also achieved this goal through the work of Ms. Sue Thurman in the editorial board of the *Aframerican Woman's Journal*. Meaning was found for Thurman's personal life as he implemented his goal for unity within the church and in the community. He underscored the significance of this personal experience, this coming to the understanding and realization of oneself by stating the following:

> The communal growth and development of Fellowship Church marked also my own personal pilgrimage. The unfolding of the pattern here was the scenario by which I was working out the meaning of my own life. In the validation of the idea, I would find validation for myself. All programs, projects, and such were as windows through which my spiritual landscape could be seen and sensed. This qualitative experience I sought for all who shared in the Fellowship community—a search for the moment when God appeared in the head, heart, and soul of the worshipper. This was the moment above all moments, intimate, personal, private, yet shared, miraculously, with the whole human family in celebration.[51]

Thurman's extended "human family," his beloved church, promoted change and acted as a clearinghouse for social transformation by means of genuine spirituality. He and the membership were always encouraged to take personal responsibility for social change. His theology of reconciliation and unity served to alleviate the tensions of a conflicted era brought on by political ideologies of totalitarian dictatorship and the counter democratic revolution of allied countries, like the United States. As he stated, it was by special grace that Fellowship Church emerged at a historic moment in world crisis created by the struggle between totalitarianism and democracy.

Thurman's life is not only defined by his many accomplishments in social, racial, and consciousness; the church also achieved this goal through the work of Ms. Sue Thurman in the religious terms, but also by the fact that he lived as a black man in a predominantly white society, a society he transformed with his theology of love and inclusion. His beloved church lived the gospel it preached. As a result, he impacted modern theology and race relations as to reflect the love of God and the unity of humankind.

Thurman's model for racial unity has inspired this project, whose main focus is centered around racial reconciliation through oneness in the love of Christ. Reconciliation is, in fact, a major component in these days of conflict and tension. It is not only the most intelligent goal to be pursued; it is also a Christian duty. In this context, the church should play a leading role in the promotion of racial harmony. Reconciliation through the intervention of the church is significant in that it opposes subjugation. As Wallace B. Clift states, "religion has always been the instrument or arm of social protest. For Moses and Martin Luther King Jr., it was the rallying cry for liberation from social oppression."[52] The model for racial reconciliation being underscored in this dissertation is a result of my understanding of Thurman's and DeYoung's work. It considers the following steps for interaction and fellowship with other denominations and people to promote unity and understanding. In order for this spiritual interaction to occur, one must believe that God can transform the most hopeless relationships into deep and loving friendships. Emphasis should also be put on fellowship to promote the model being discussed here.

Besides fellowship with people of other cultures, races, and backgrounds, one should also consider the following pragmatic steps toward achieving race reconciliation within the church:

1. Prayer Meetings (To be held weekly at 6:00 a.m. and 6:00 p.m. in the church's sanctuary)
2. Outreach through Unity Rallies (March to promote racial peace)
3. Making the First Move (Inviting components of the neighborhood and the community at large to church worship hour and social gatherings)
4. Visiting the Sick (in nursing homes and hospitals)
5. Establishing a Prison Ministry (Weekly visitation of local jails)
6. Providing Shelter (To assist battered women, abused children, and the homeless)
7. Psychological and Spiritual Counseling (For the downtrodden and brokenhearted)
8. Youth Conventions (Forming a youth caucus to promote interaction within the races)
9. Mass Demonstrations (To emphasize the importance of racial unity within the community and the nation)
10. Money Management and Debt Alleviation (For members of the church and community)

Once this model is implemented, one can feel hopeful that the love that unites Christ to humankind can be the same love that unites the human race. It is by God's grace that such an accomplishment is possible. Thurman's inspiration for the implementation of his model for racial unity was the love of God and his faith that love could promote understanding and bridge all gaps segregating humanity. The gospel of Christ is the model for the theology of love and social applications proposed in this study. Such a model cannot be just a theoretical one. It must be a pragmatic and tangible one. The steps proposed in this dissertation should lead to the achievement of this goal and consequently contribute to the unity of all peoples.

Furthermore, in the same manner as displayed by Thurman's model for racial unity, fellowship with spirituality must be practiced and preached to impact the way we live and to change the unfair nature of the present social structures. Spirituality must be considered when addressing these questions of racial injustice. Spirituality offers alternatives to the destructive forces of racial discrimination. It should be a priority in the twenty-first century when dealing with issues of race, race reconciliation, and peace. Individual and collective agendas should strive to demand and promote equality of rights and understanding of individual differences. Just as racism exists in colonized societies, so does spirituality, which should transcends race, class, gender, and nationality.

This project was meaningful in that it afforded a better understanding of white supremacy and racism worldwide. It also gave hope that spirituality is the cure for this sickness. The writers who inspired this work offer solutions for social, economic, educational, political, and spiritual progress. The civil rights movement and the Million Man March affirm that there is power in unity, and that God is in control and cares for the plight of oppressed people everywhere.

Does America really want racial reconciliation? I agree with Fredrick Douglass. America wants the crop without the agitation. A friend of mine, who is white, states that "most whites believe they want racial reconciliation until it affects them. When they realize that they must share their privileges, they have second thoughts." Based on my experience, the idealist side of me is optimistic about racial reconciliation because there has been progress made in race relations. We, as humans, want to do right. However, the realist side of me is pessimistic because of sin, selfishness, and pride. Most people are concerned about themselves first and others second. Most of all racism is still the common denominator of America's problem.

In addition, I feel that most blacks and whites avoid the subject of race relations because it is a touchy subject. As a result, most races wear masks or fake fellowship with each other. Often, we know what needs to be said to one another, but our fears prevent blacks and whites from speaking truth. The Bible tells us to "speak the truth in love" (Eph 4:15). I feel that most blacks and whites remain superficial because we are afraid of conflict; whenever an issue regarding race comes up that might cause tension or discomfort, it is immediately glossed over in order to preserve or present a false sense of peace or false united front.

Moreover, I asked myself, "How can I achieve racial reconciliation?" First, I must look to the model of the civil rights movement. For instance, Dr. King and others used nonviolence as a means to end legal segregation. They were committed to nonviolence, prayer, scripture, and love. He felt that even though nonviolence may be perceived as cowardly, it is not. He and I believe believed that racial tension existed between good and evil and not between people and that our only means of survival is to love one another, which comes from scripture and the teachings of Jesus. I agree with this teaching and philosophy. I also believe that in order for individuals to love those who hate them, we must utilize three pledges: (1) The Pledge of Allegiance to the American flag. (2) The Million Man March (3) The pledge to the Ministry of Reconciliation. (2 Cor 5:18)

Secondly, I must seek the good in everyone. It is vital that we look within and realize that in the best of us there is some evil and in the worst of us there is some good. For this reason, we must follow scriptures about love and do the unnatural, and that is "to love them that hate you and bless them that curse you" (Luke 6:27–31). According to the Gospel of Luke 6:27–31, Jesus gives a command that is unnatural. He commanded us as Christians to love our enemies, do good to those who hate us, bless those who curse us, and pray for those who mistreat us. I realize that this is stunning and an ordinary person cannot do this because from the natural point of view, loving an enemy or seeking the good who hate us is strange, yet Jesus calls those who follow him to live and go beyond normal and natural expectations because this action demonstrates the Ministry of Reconciliation.

Finally, I feel that it's time for truth because the truth will set blacks and whites free. Let's stop telling lies, stop pretending and faking, and be honest, because we are all connected by the hand of God. Until we care enough to confront and resolve the underlying barriers, we will never grow close to each other. For this reason, I care enough about America to speak truth even when it is easier to remain silent and pretend all is well. By speaking truth, we are learning from each other, but most importantly we are growing and learning about ourselves. Does America want racial reconciliation? I say yes because America is ready for change.

Endnotes

1. *No Longer Invisible: Afro-Latin Americans Today.* London, England: Minority Rights Group, 1995.
2. The Holy Bible: *New International Version*, 1 Corinthians 13: 4–7.
3. *The Holy Bible: New International Version*, 1 Peter 3:1, 1 Peter 4: 14–16, Romans 13: 3–4.
4. *The Holy Bible: New International Version*, Romans 8:28.
5. *The Holy Bible: New International Version*, Luke 14:11.
6. *The Holy Bible: New International Version*, John 1:1–4, Romans 1:2–5, 1 John 1:1–3.
7. *The Holy Bible: New International Version*, John 1:1–4, Romans 1:2–5, 1 John 1:1–3.
8. *The Holy Bible: New International Version*, John 5:18.
9. *The Holy Bible: New International Version*, John 5:8.

10. *The South and Christian Ethics.*
11. *Kelsey, Racism and Christian Understanding, 33.*
12. Kelsey, George. *Racism and Christian Understanding of Man*, 87.
13. King Jr., Martin L. *Where Do We Go From Here*, 69. op. cit.
14. West, Cornel. *Race Matters*, 15.
15. West, Cornel. *Race Matters*, 23.
16. Roberts, J. Deotis. *Liberation and Reconciliation*, 59.
17. *Morris in DeYoung, Curtis P. Coming Together, 6.*
18. *The Holy Bible*: *New International Version*, Acts 2:44–47.
19. Cone in Martin and Malcolm and America, 62.
20. Cone, *Martin and Malcolm and America*, 62.
21. Lincoln, Eric. *Martin Luther King Jr.*, 25.
22. Cone, James H. *Martin and Malcolm and America*, 77.
23. Cone, James H. *Martin and Malcolm and America*, 78.
24. Cone, James H. *Martin and Malcolm and America*, 58.
25. Cone, James H. *Martin and Malcolm and America*, 84.
26. Cone, James H. *Martin and Malcolm and America*, 85.
27. Cone, James H. *Martin and Malcolm and America*, 98.
28. Cone, James H. *Martin and Malcolm and America*, 99.
29. Cone, James H. *Martin and Malcolm and America*, 99.
30. Gallen, David. *Malcolm As They Knew Him*, 53.
31. Cone, James H. *Martin and Malcolm and America*, 155.
32. Gallen, David. *Malcolm As They Knew Him*, 113–130.
33. Gallen, David. *Malcolm As They Knew Him*, 186.
34. *The Holy Bible: King James Version*, Luke 4:18–19.
35. Siberman in Cone, *Black Theology and Black Power* 10.
36. Cone, James H. *Black Theology and Black Power*, 5.

37. Baker-Fletcher, Garth K. *Black Religion after the Million Man March*, 103.
38. DeYoung, Curtiss Paul. *Reconciliation*, xvi.
39. Thurman, Howard. *With Head and Heart*, 142.
40. Thunnan Howard, *With Head and Heart*, 143.
41. Thurman, Howard. *With Head and Heart*, 143.
42. Thurman, Howard. *With Head and Heart*, 143.
43. Thurman, Howard. *With Head and Heart*, 144.
44. Thurman, Howard. *With Head and Heart*,
45. Thurman, Howard. *With Head and Heart*,
46. Thurman, Howard. *With Head and Heart*,
47. Thurman, Howard. *With Head and Heart*, 146.
48. Thurman, Howard. *With Head and Heart*, 147.
49. Thurman, Howard. *With Head and Heart*, 148.
50. Thurman, Howard. *With Head and Heart*, 158.
51. Thurman, Howard. *With Head and Heart*, 159.
52. Clift, Wallace B. *Jung and Christianity*, 68.

Bibliography

Battle, Michael. Reconciliation: The Ubunty Theology of Desmond Tutu. Cleveland, Ohio: The Pilgrim Press. 1997.

Gwen, Cashmore and Joan Puls. Clearing the Way. Geneva, Switzerland: WCC Publications, World Council of Churches, 1990.

Chiba, Shin et, al. Christian Ethics in Ecumenical Context. Grand Rapids, Michigan: Wm. B. Eerdmans Publishing Co., 1995.

Cleage, Albert Jr. The Black Messiah: Kansas City, Missouri: Sheed Andrews and McMeel, Inc. Clift, Wallace B. Jung and Christianity. New York, New York: Crossroad Publishing Company, 1982.

Cochrane, James et. al. *Facing the Truth: South African Faith Communities and the Truth and Reconciliation Commission.* Athens, Ohio: Ohio University Press, 1999.

Cone, James H. *Martin & Malcolm & America.* Maryknoll, New York: Otbis Books, 1993.

—*Black Theology and Black Power.* New York, New York: Harper San Francisco, 1989.

—*Black Theology of Liberation*: Maryknoll, New York: Orbis Books, 1986.

Crow Jr., Paul A. *Christian Unity: Matrix for Mission.* New York, New York: Friendship Press, 1952.

DeYoung, Curtis Paul. *Coming Together: The Bible's Message in an Age of Diversity*: Valley Forge, Pennsylvania: Judson Press, 1995.

—*Reconciliation.* Valley Forge, Pennsylvania: Judson Press, 1995.

Douglass, Kelly Brown. *The Black Christ*: Maryknoll, New York: Orbis Books, 1994.

Erskine, Noel. *King Among The Theologians*: Cleveland, Ohio: The Pilgrim Press, 1994.

Fackre, Gabriel. *Ecumenical Faith in Evangelical Perspective.* Grand Rapids, Michigan: William B. Eerdmans Publishing Company, 1993.

Frazier, E. Franklin. *Black Bourgeoisie.* New York: Macmillan Publishing Company, 1962.

Fulop, Timothy B., and Raboteau, Albert J. *African-American Religion*: New York, New York: Routledge, 1997.

Gallen, David. *Malcolm As They Knew Him*: New York, New York: Carrol & Graf Publishers, 1992.

Guillaurnin, Colette. *Racism, Sexism, Power and Ideology*: London: Routledge, 1995.

Hadden, Jeffrey K. *Gideon's Gang: A Case Study of the Church in Social Action.* Philadelphia, Pennsylvania: United Church Press, 1974.

Haley, Alex, *The Autobiography of Malcolm X:* New York, New York: Ballantine Books, 1965.

Harding, Vincent. *Martin Luther King The Inconvenient Hero*: Maryknoll, New York: Orbis Books, 1997.

Hardy, James Earl. *Spike Lee*: New York, New York: Chelsea House Publishers, 1996.

Harkness, Georgia. *The Ministry of Reconciliation*. Nashville, Tennessee: Abingdon Press, 1971.

Hinson, B. Glenn. *Spirituality in Ecumenical Perspective.* Louisville, Kentucky: John Knox Press, 1993.

Hooks, Bell. *Reel to Real.* New York, New York: Routledge, 1996.

James R o. *Christianity and Other Religions*: New York. New York: I. B. Lippincott Company, 1986.

Johnson Publishing Company, "Robert Townsend" Jet, August 9, 1993 v84 n15 p58.

Kane, J. Herbert. *Wanted: World Christians:* Grand Rapids, Michigan: Baker Book House Company, 1986.

Kelsey, George. *Racism and Christian Understanding of Man:* New York, New York: Charles Scribner's Son, 1956.

King Jr., Martin L. *Where Do We Go From Here: Chaos or Community:* New York: Harper & Row Publishers, 1967.

King, Antie. *Country of My Skull: Guilt, Sorrow, And the Limits of Forgiveness in the New South Africa:* New York, New York: Times Books Random House, 1998.

Kyle, Haselden. *The Racial Problem in Christian Perspective*: New York, New York: Harper & Row, 1959.

Lincoln, Eric. *Martin Luther King Jr.: A Profile:* New York, New York: IIIII and Wang, 1970.

Macdonald, Donald Stone. *The Koreans: Contemporary Politics and Society*: London, Paris: Westview Press, 198.

Martin, Ralph P. *Reconciliation: A Study of Paul's Theology*. Atlanta, Georgia; John Knox Press, 1981.

Meler, August and Rudwick, Elliott. *Black Protest in the Sixties*: Chicago, Illinois: Quadrangle Books, 1970.

Melendy, H. Brett. *Asians in America*: New York, New York: Hippocrene Books, 1977.

Meredith, Martin. Coming to Terms: *South Africa's Search for Truth*. New York, New York; Public Affairs, 1999.

Perkins, Ken Parish. "Mo Better, But Still Not That Good." *Dallas Morning News*, 2June 1991.

Petrakis, John, "B.A.P.S." Means Brainless and Probably Scriptless. *Chicago Tribune*, 28 March, 1997.

Osgood, Cornelius. *The Koreans and Their Culture*: New York, New York: The Ronald Press Company, 1951.

Reid, Mark A. *Spike Lee's Do the Right Thing*: Cambridge, Massachusetts: Cambridge University Press.

Roberts, J. Deotis. *Liberation and Reconciliation: A Black Theology*: Philadelphia, Pennsylvania: The Westminster Press, 1971.

Sande, Ken. *The Peacemaker: A Biblical Guide to Resolving Personal Conflict*, Grand Rapids, Michigan: Baker Books, 1997.

Sanders, Cheryl J. *Saints in Exile: The Holiness-Pentecostal Experience in African American Religion and Culture*. New York, New York: Oxford University Press, 1996.

Snyder, T. Richards. *Divided We Fall: Moving from Suspicion to Solidarity*, Louisville, Kentucky: John Knox Press, 1992.

Sugirtharajah, R. S. *Asians Faces of Jesus*: Maryknoll, New York: Oris Books, 1993.

The Holy Bible. New King James Version. Thomas Nelson Company, 1982.

Thorogood, Bernard. *One Wind, Many Flames: Church Unity and the Diversity of the Churches*. Geneva, Switzerland: WCC Publication, World Council of Churches, 1991.

Thurman, Howard. *The Luminous Darkness*: New York, New York: Harper & Row, 1965.

—*With Head and Heart*. New York, New York: Harcourt Brace & Company, 1979.

Torrance, Thomas F. *Theology in Reconciliation*. Grand Rapids, Michigan: William B. Eerdmans Publishing Company, 1976.

Usami, Koshi. *Somatic Comprehension of Unity: The Church in Ephesus*. Tokyo, Japan: Biblical Institute Press, 1983.

U.S. Commission on Civil Rights, *Civil Rights Issues Facing Asian Americans in the 1990's,* February 1992.

Vieira, Rosangela Maria. "Brazil" In *No Longer Invisible: Afro-Latin Americans Today*: London, England: Minority Rights Group, 1995.

Volf, Miroslav. *Exclusion and Embrace*. Nashville, Tennessee: Abingdon Press, 1 991.

Watkins, Craig S. *Representing*: Chicago, Illinois: The University of Chicago Press, 1998.

Wiley, Ralph. *Best Seat In The House*: New York, New York: Crown Publishers, 1994.

Weiner, Michael. *The Origins of the Koreans Community*: Atlantic Highlands, New Jersey: Humanities Press International, 1989.

West, Comel. Race Matters: New York, New York: Vintage Books, 1994.

Wijngaards, John. *Together in my Name*. Mahwah, New Jersey: Paulist Press, 1995.

Wilmore, Gayraud S. *Black Religion and Black Radicalism*: Maryknoll, New York: Orbis Books, 1983.

Young, Andrew. *The Spiritual Memoirs of Andrew Young*: Nashville, Tennessee: Thomas Nelson Publishers, 1994.